Decorative Designs in
Hardanger

MILNER CRAFT SERIES

Decorative Designs in
Hardanger

GINA MARION

SALLY MILNER PUBLISHING

First published in 1998 by
Sally Milner Publishing Pty Ltd
RMB 54 Burra Road
Burra Creek NSW 2620
Australia

© Gina Marion, 1998

Designed by Anna Warren, Warren Ventures, Sydney
Photography by Ben Wrigley, Melbourne
Stitch diagrams by Don Bradford
Printed in Hong Kong

National Library of Australia Cataloguing-in-Publication data:

Marion, Gina.
 Decorative designs in hardanger

ISBN 1 86351 214 4.

1. Hardanger needlework - Patterns. I. Title. (Series:
Milner craft series).

746.44

Dedication

I dedicate this book to my mum, Jan Laut, who has always supported and encouraged my love of embroidery and helped me with new ideas and problems when they have arisen.

CONTENTS

ACKNOWLEDGEMENTS

During the preparation of this book, I have been fortunate to have support and help from several people. I would like to thank Sally Milner for her support and the opportunity to write a second book; Jenny Bradford for her encouragement and permission to use embroidery techniques from several of her books; and Don Bradford for drawing my diagrams.

My thanks to Julie Hanks from Mudgee for her hand dyed Gumnut silks and Blossoms wools; Elizabeth White from Downunder Designs for Watercolour and Wildflower threads and fabric; Jennifer Newman for her beautiful Minnamurra threads; to Ireland Needlecraft for the wooden pincushion and blue china trinket bowl; and to my father, Peter Laut, who made the wooden embroidery box. Last, but certainly not least, is StitchCraft, who supplied me with the computer software for designing my graphs.

INTRODUCTION

Hardanger embroidery has had a revival during the last few years. For those who have not attempted this type of embroidery before, it is an extension of forms of embroidery, such as cross stitch, where the fabric threads are counted for the placement of the stitching and a graph is used as a guide. In this book, for the larger embroideries, only one quarter of the graph is given, and for some of the smaller projects, the complete graph is given.

The most common stitch used for hardanger is satin stitch, which is used extensively, and buttonhole stitch which is used for the edging, which is described in two different forms, depending on the type of edging you prefer. Several types of decorative stitches are used to make the embroidery more interesting. Needleweaving is a part of hardanger and can be used to great effect to achieve what looks like handmade lace.

Hardanger embroidery was designed during the late seventeenth century when lace from Europe was not available to the majority of people. It is traditional that the embroidery is white on white or cream on cream. I have used coloured fabric and threads for many of the projects in this book. We have many coloured fabrics and threads available to us today which makes the choice a little harder but the results can be fabulous. It is worth experimenting with colour to see what effects can be obtained, from something dainty to something quite bold. The use of extras like beads and metallic threads add a point of interest to the embroidery and can make a fairly ordinary piece of embroidery look spectacular.

Although I love the traditional hardanger, I also enjoy the challenge of using coloured fabric and threads. It is lovely to experiment with coloured threads, but especially the variegated threads that are available on the market today. There are many different types and weights of threads available and each has its own personality in colour and texture. Always try different weight fabric and threads together to see what result you can achieve.

The last chapter in this book deals with designing your own hardanger patterns. Part of designing your own embroideries is choosing the colour of the fabric and threads. It might sound scary to try, but is worth the effort. I always find new fabric and threads will lead my mind to ideas that might not otherwise have occurred to me.

CHAPTER 1

GETTING STARTED

This chapter is all about getting started on a hardanger project. There are a few necessities that are essential for this type of embroidery. There are also steps that are necessary before each embroidery can be undertaken.

Always buy the best quality fabric and threads that you can afford. The use of poorer quality essentials can destroy all the work and time you are about to put into what should be a family heirloom. The difference will always show in the end result.

BEFORE YOU BEGIN

Before any project is started, there are two steps that should always be undertaken:

1. Cut the fabric to the required size and then overlock or zigzag the edges to prevent fraying. Fray Stopper is a product which has been developed to prevent fraying and works quite well. It can be used as an alternative to overlocking or zigzagging.
2. Using a contrasting thread, mark the horizontal and vertical centre lines with basting or tacking stitches. This step is important, as it gives you a clear guide, dividing the embroidery into quarters like the graph you will be using.

ORDER OF WORK

The stitching on each project should be done in the following order:

1. The satin stitching.
2. The eyelets.
3. The blanket stitching.
4. The needleweaving and extra embroidery stitching, bullion and detached button-hole stitches, and stitching using metallic thread and the attaching of beads.

Only after all these stitches are complete should cutting around the edge be contemplated and then completed. Otherwise some of the stitching may pull out fabric threads as you embroider, especially the eyelet stitching.

THREADS

I have used many types and colours of threads in this book chosen from the great variety of threads and fabric available on the market today. As a guide I have given a list of suppliers in the back of the book. Most are retail outlets where I buy my supplies but most are happy to fill mail orders for you. But check out your local suppliers as well, as they may have some unusual materials and threads available which are equally suitable.

Coton Perle

This is a cotton thread which is available in sizes 3,5,8 and 12. The higher the number, the finer the thread: no. 5 is fairly thick and no. 12 is fine. It is made in France and is used extensively for hardanger embroidery. It comes in a variety of colours which can be used alone or in conjunction with other types and colours of threads. For the work in this book I used coton perle no. 8 and no. 12 extensively. The size of the thread you use depends on the fabric used. Heavier fabric such as Lugana needs coton perle no. 5 for the satin and buttonhole stitching and then no. 8 for the finer stitching and needleweaving. For fabric such as the Belfast linen, coton perle no. 8 is used for the satin and buttonhole stitching and no. 12 for the other stitches.

The rule for stitching is the thicker thread is used for the satin and buttonhole stitching and the finer thread is used for the finer details of the embroidery and the needleweaving,

Coton perle threads have a shiny lustre which contrasts nicely with the matt finish of the fabric.

Watercolour and Wildflower Threads

Watercolour threads are equivalent to the coton perle no. 5. Wildflower threads are equivalent to the coton perle no. 8. These hand painted threads come from the United States of America. They are multi-coloured thread with four or five colours on each thread. They come in a huge range of colourways from soft subtle colours to bright vibrant colours. The Watercolour and Wildflower colours all match so it is possible to work the complete embroidery in the same set of colours. Alternatively, they can be mixed and matched with plain colours which will compliment the colourways of the variegation.

As with all variegated threads, it is necessary to buy enough skeins to complete the embroidery because the dye lots may vary.

With the more stringent environmental laws in the USA now, the chemical fixatives that were used to stop the dyes from running can no longer be used. Therefore, it is necessary to wash these threads in cold water with a little salt or vinegar added.

Minnamurra Threads

These threads are variegated with two colours on each thread. They come in 6 strands, and coton perle no. 5 and no. 8. They are DMC threads which are hand dyed in Australia.

For some of the work in this book I have used a combination of the stranded and the coton perle for a special effect. The stranded is used for adding embroidered flowers to the hardanger embroidery in the same colours to produce a lovely subtle effect.

Minnamurra threads come in twenty different colourways. Again, make sure enough threads are bought to complete the embroidery as the dye lots may vary.

Spring

These threads are the equivalent to coton perle no. 5. I have used them for the Christmas decorations. They have a shiny and a matt thread woven together to give an interesting effect on the decorations, just a touch of highlight to add interest.

Silk Ribbon

I have used 2 mm silk ribbon for the embroidered Flannel Flowers on one of the doilies. The silk ribbon comes in a variety of widths but I have used this size to make delicate flowers to complement the embroidery. I have also used a 4 mm ribbon which is slightly variegated on two of the smaller projects. It gives a subtle effect to the embroidery.

Silk ribbon is available at most craft stores and embroidery shops.

Metallic Thread

I have used a small amount of metallic threads for some of the items of this book. I have used three types, one from DMC, one from Madeira and the other is a Kreinik thread.

Each metallic thread is different in pliability so each has been used for a different purpose. The DMC metallic is a strong thread and has been used for embroidering eyelets. The Kreinek thread has been used for working outline stitching to highlight satin stitched shapes. The Madeira thread has been used along the borders of the shawl.

Metallic threads can be a bit difficult to use because the thread is not smooth like a cotton or silk thread, so be careful and patient to get a good result.

Gumnut Yarns

The Gumnut Yarns I have used are silk and matching shades of wool. The silks, Blossoms, are a delight to use. They are not liable to wear as much as the coton perle and keep their lustre to the end of the thread. They are equivalent to coton perle no. 8. I have used them in various projects. They are slightly variegated in soft subtle colours.

I have also used the wools, Gemstones, for the shawl where I have used two shades of each colour to give the embroidery a lovely effect. I had to use two strands of the wool to give good cover over the Afghan fabric.

NEEDLES

I have used a variety of needles for the embroidered articles in this book. Where there is a combination of hardanger and other types of embroidery, it is necessary to change the type of needle being used. Each needle has its purpose and it is much easier to use the correct needle to get the required result.

coton perle no. 5	use tapestry needle no. 24
coton perle no. 8 and 12	use tapestry needle no. 26
silk ribbon	use chenille needle no. 18
beads	use beading needle
stranded threads	use milliners needle
metallic threads	use tapestry needle no. 24

These are the needles I use, but if you have trouble using them, try changing the size until you find a needle you are comfortable with and which gives you the results you want.

The tapestry needles have a blunt end which makes it easier for ensuring that the needle goes between the threads of the fabric not through them. The chenille needle is similar to the tapestry needle but has a sharp point. I have only used it for the silk ribbon embroidery. The beading needles are long and fine. They are necessary to pick up and attach the beads. A fine embroidery needle is an alternative to the beading needle. Because they are so fine, it is sometimes hard to thread, so I use a quilting thread which is waxed as it is stiff and holds the point. Milliners or straw needles are used for embroidering bullion and detached buttonhole stitch. They are very necessary because each needle has the same diameter along the length of the shaft which makes it easier to pull the needle through with all the wraps or buttonhole stitches on it.

SCISSORS

Scissors are an important tool for hardanger embroidery. It is necessary to possess a fine small pair of scissors. As well as cutting the threads, it is also necessary to cut the fabric threads, and this requires a fine sharp blade. I use what are commonly known as Stork scissors. I find them very useful for this type of work, but a fine pair of nail scissors also works just as well. A blunt pair of scissors is next to useless and leaves fluffy ends where you cut the fabric threads instead of a clean cut, so make sure yours are sharp.

HOOPS

An embroidery hoop should be used for hardanger embroidery unless you feel that you can control the tension of the fabric and thread. I would recommend the use of the hoop for beginners as the correct tension can be hard to establish. If the tension is too tight, then the fabric will pucker and ruin the effort of the embroidery. If the tension is loose, it will not hold the fabric threads comfortably when they are cut. It is most necessary to use the hoop for embroidering the satin and buttonhole stitching. It is not as necessary to use the hoop for the needleweaving. Either a wooden or spring loaded hoop is satisfactory to use.

BEADS

I have used Mill Hill Beads for some of the projects. They are made of glass and come in small packs containing approximately 200 beads in each pack. They come in a variety of colours, shapes and sizes. There are small, large and bugle beads which come in a variety of common and antique colours. They are a delight to use. Use the beading needle to attach them to the fabric. I usually use a thread which is the colour of the background fabric to attach them, using a half cross stitch.

FABRIC

I have used a variety of fabrics which are all readily available. I have used different types of fabric depending on the effect I wanted to achieve for the finished article.

I use Lugana, which comes in a variety of colours, from cream and white to a dark blue and crimson. The Lugana is a mixture of cotton and polyester and is easy on the hands to use. It is 26 threads to the inch, or 10 threads per centimetre.

Linda is a pure cotton fabric and is 28 threads to the inch, or 11 threads to the centimetre.

Jobelan is made from cotton and modal, a manmade fibre, and is a lovely soft fabric to use. Jobelan is also 28 threads to the inch, or 11 threads to the centimetre.

I have also used Belfast linen, a pure linen, which is 32 threads per inch, or 14 threads per centimetre.

In this book, I have also used a piece of Afghan fabric which comes in a set size piece and is available in white or cream and may have a border design in the weave. It has 22 threads per inch, or 6 threads per centimetre.

MAGNIFYING GLASS

Magnifying glasses have become readily available over the last few years. Some of my students find it is much easier to see the fabric and threads while embroidering if they use their magnifying glasses. Hardanger, or any type of counted thread work, is a good test for the eyesight. If you can't see the fabric well enough, try a magnifying glass. There are several types available: magnifying glasses, a magnifying glass which you can hang around your neck, and also the floor stand types of magnifiers which have a light attached.

Something I also find very useful is a Craft globe which is available from most good electrical stores. This globe is made of a transparent blue glass and gives a daylight light which is excellent to embroider under. They come in both 60 and 100 watts.

The Designs

Each project in this books comes with a graphed design. All hardanger designs are depicted on graphs. For larger projects, usually only a quarter of each graphed design is necessary, as it is repeated on each quarter of the fabric to complete the whole embroidery. For the smaller designs I have given a complete graph.

The graph lines represent the fabric threads and the heavier, short lines, represent the embroidery.

Note that the embroidery threads are actually placed between the fabric threads to form the patterns so you are not sewing through the fabric threads as with most embroidery. Where there is a blank space on a graph, it means a number of threads have been cut and withdrawn.

Care of Hardanger Embroidery

As with all hand embroidered articles, it is paramount to keep the embroidery as clean as possible at all times. If the embroidered article becomes dirty while embroidering it, wash it when it is finished. Always make sure your hands are clean before embroidering. Keep the embroidery away from open fires and heaters and cover when you are not embroidering.

If it is necessary to wash the embroidery, wash in lukewarm water and use a gentle detergent or soap. Do not rub or wring the embroidery or it will make the embroidery thread fluffy. Rinse in clean lukewarm water. Press out as much water as possible and then lay flat on a towel and roll it up. Squeeze the towel gently, unroll it and place the embroidery on a rack to dry. Do not place in direct sunlight. When the embroidery is dry, place it face down on a dry towel on an ironing board. Place a piece of cloth, such as a man's handkerchief, over the embroidery and then carefully iron the embroidery flat with a relatively hot iron. The piece of cloth prevents the embroidery being scorched. Ironing directly on top of the embroidery will flatten the work and will detract from the finished article.

SUMMARY OF HINTS

- Always finish the edges of the fabric before starting to embroider.
- Mark the horizontal and vertical centres of the fabric with a coloured thread as a guide for the embroidery placement.
- Photocopy the graph to save the book from being damaged with continual use.
- Enlarge the graph on a photocopier if you have trouble reading it.
- Make sure the needles you use still have the shiny coating on them.
- Use small scissors with sharp blades and points.
- Use a thimble as it can saves holes in your finger.
- Buy enough of each thread to complete the whole project.
- Attach a ribbon through the handles of the scissors. Hang them around your neck and then they are less likely to be lost.
- Have a good light source when embroidering — a window during the day or a lamp during the evening.
- Use a magnifying glass when embroidering if you have trouble seeing the fabric threads.
- Never use a thread longer than 30 cm (12 in), especially if it is the coton perle.
- Only use a 26 cm (10 in) length of silk ribbon when embroidering.
- Use a hoop if you have problems keeping the tension even.
- Do not cut the fabric threads that are to be withdrawn when you are tired.
- Always put the embroidery away when finished so it stays clean.
- Save the colour band from each thread with a sample of the thread attached to it.
- Pulling the needle towards you is much easier than pushing the needle away from you.
- If the thread unravels on the needle while embroidering, twist is up again.
- Use a marking pen that can be erased, or which will fade, for flower stitch guides.
- Use quilting thread for attaching beads.
- Beads or small pearls can be used instead of colonial knots to give a shimmery finish to the embroidery.
- Wash any embroidery using the variegated threads in cold water with salt or vinegar to act as a mordent.
- When you have finished the embroidery, place face down on a padded ironing board and iron with a man's handkerchief over the top.

CHAPTER 2

STITCHES

KLOSTER BLOCKS

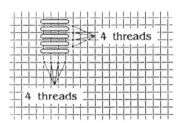

Kloster blocks are the basis of hardanger embroidery. Each block is always five satin stitches over four threads. This never varies.

This stitch is worked with the thicker of the two coton perle threads that are used: coton perle no. 5 on the Lugana and coton perle no. 8 on the Belfast linen.

Kloster blocks are embroidered in two different ways:

1. on the diagonal.
2. in a straight line.

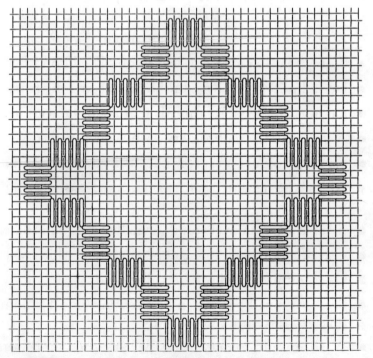

Kloster blocks on the diagonal

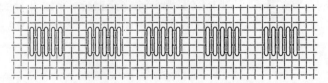

Kloster blocks in a straight line

Kloster blocks may be worked from left to right or right to left. Each block consists of five satin stitches, always worked from the bottom to the top of the block. This gives each block an even look.

BLOCKS ON THE DIAGONAL
Kloster blocks are usually worked on the diagonal of the fabric to outline the design being used.

- Starting at 1, work five satin stitches, following the numbered stitch order in the diagram.
- To make the second block, count four fabric threads to the left of the 10. Push the needle through at 11, take the needle back to 10 and pull the needle through. Complete in the same way as the first block.
- To make the third block, after completing stitch 19 to 20, take the needle back through 19 and come up to the front. Count four threads up from 19 and take the needle through to the back at 22 and come up at 23.

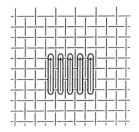

Arrows indicate the direction of the stitch

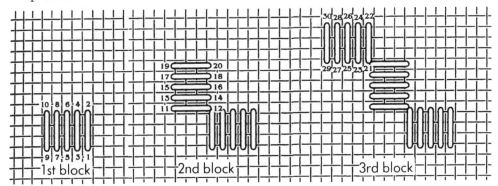

The hole in each corner is shared with the next block. If the back looks like the diagram shown, the stitching has been done incorrectly. There should be no jumping diagonally from one block to the next.

The back should look like this.

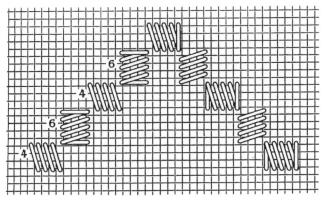

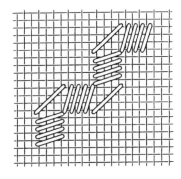

Back of work — wrong

Back of work — right

The stitching on the back should be on an angle and alternate blocks of 4 and 6 stitches on the diagonal.

BLOCKS IN A STRAIGHT LINE
The first block is embroidered in the same way as the first block embroidered on the diagonal.

When that is completed, count over four threads from the bottom right corner of the first block. This is the starting point of the second block.

This process is repeated to make a straight line of kloster blocks. The back of the embroidery should look like the top diagram, not the lower one. If the stitching has been done the wrong way, the blocks will not sit correctly.

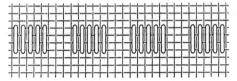

Front of work

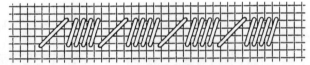

Back of work — right

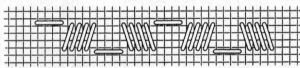

Back of work — wrong

It is critical that the blocks are correctly embroidered because the satin stitch edge is where the fabric is cut. If the stitching is done incorrectly, then there is nothing to hold the fabric threads in place when they are cut.

STARTING AND FINISHING A THREAD
When starting a thread, tie a knot in the end. Take the needle through the fabric from the top to the bottom approximately 8 cm (3 in) from the starting point. Start and complete the kloster blocks with the thread.

To end the thread, run it back and forth three times under the last kloster block, catching the fabric with the needle. Now go back to the beginning of the thread. Cut off the knot, thread the needle with the cut end and finish it in the same way as for the end of the thread. This process is known as 'a waste knot'.

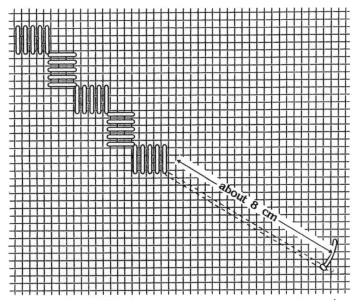

Starting a thread   waste knot

EYELETS

Eyelets are decorative stitches that can be used by themselves, between two rows of kloster blocks or between a row of kloster blocks and a row of buttonhole stitches. If the eyelets are used in conjunction with buttonhole stitching, then the eyelets must be embroidered before cutting around the buttonhole edging or the fabric threads will pull out.

Eyelets are worked in the finer coton perle thread, usually the coton perle no. 8 or no. 12.

There must be 4 x 4 threads in the centre of two rows of kloster blocks to be able to embroider an eyelet.

- Coming up at A, take the needle through the centre and bring it up at B. Pull the stitch tight.
- Go down through the centre again and come up at C. Pull the stitch tight.
- Repeat this process until stitches have been sewn into all the satin stitches of each kloster block.

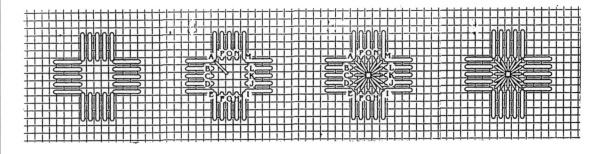

The tighter the thread is pulled after each stitch, the larger the hole becomes in the centre. It is much easier to make a hole by going down through the centre instead of coming up through the centre. If one stitch lies on top of the previous stitch, pull the thread tighter so that it lies flat against the fabric.

When moving from one eyelet to the next, run the thread under the kloster blocks on the back. Make sure the starting point is always in the same place on each kloster block.

Anchor the ends of each thread by running back and forth three times under the closest kloster block, catching the fabric threads.

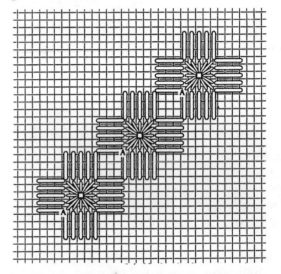

ALGERIAN EYELETS

Algerian eyelets are used for the same reason as eyelets and they can also be used for decorative purposes. They are done with either a coton perle no. 8 or no. 12. If they are done in conjunction with a buttonhole edge, they must be embroidered before cutting.

- Starting at A (the first stitch of a kloster block), bring the needle up from underneath the fabric.
- Find the centre and take the needle down through it and come back up at B (the centre stitch of the group of five for a kloster block).
- Go down through the centre again and come up at C (the last stitch of the kloster block).
- Repeat the process until the eyelet is completed.

Start each Algerian eyelet at the same corner with each block. Run the thread underneath the kloster blocks to reach the next block.

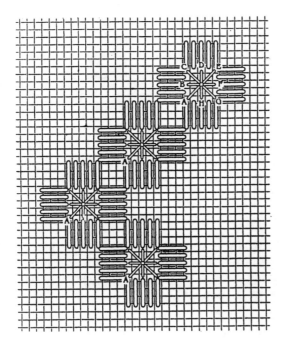

SATIN STITCH

Satin stitch is one of the most difficult stitches to do really well. It is made easier on an even-weave linen, because the fabric threads space each stitch evenly. The tension also has to be practised so that the stitches are not pulled too tightly, which causes puckering of the fabric underneath.

- To start, use a waste knot going through the fabric from the top approximately 8 cm (3 in) from the starting point A.

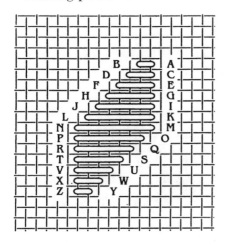

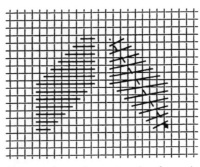

Front of work   Back of work

- Come up at A and take the needle down at B, up at C and down at D. Continue the process until the block is finished. The back should be a satin stitched block with slanted stitches. The back should never have little stitches from B to D, C to E, and so on. Incorrect stitching will make the satin stitches sit on an angle instead of sitting straight across the fabric. Always finish the whole block before finishing off the thread.

- When the thread is finished take it through to the back and run it under the last finished block. Cut the waste knot at the beginning of the thread, thread the needle with the end and run it under the first block.

CABLE AND DOUBLE CABLE STITCH

This stitch has been used extensively for the projects in this book, both as a single and a double row. It gives a lovely raised effect either way and looks good with any sort of embroidery.

A coton perle no. 8 or no. 12 is used to embroider this stitch. The stitch is done over two threads only. It is worked from left to right on the diagonal.

- For the first row of cable stitch, start with a waste knot and come up at 1.
- Count two fabric threads to the right and two fabric threads up from 1. This is 2. Take the needle down at 2 and come up two fabric threads to the left, but along the same horizontal thread. This is 3.
- Now count two fabric threads up from 2, this is 4. Take the needle at 4, back up at 5, through the same hole as for 2.
- Continue in this method until the required number of stitches has been embroidered.
- The second row of cable stitch that makes it double cable stitch, is done in the same way as the first,

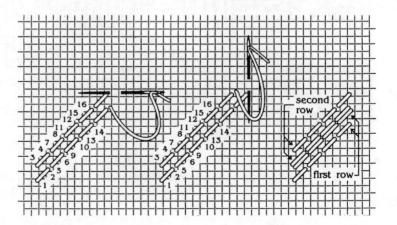

but shares the middle line of holes with the first row. The same method is used, but be careful that the new middle row does not sit on top of the first row. Corners are embroidered exactly the same way for both rows.

TURNING A CORNER

To turn a corner, an extra stitch has to be made to compensate for the turn.

- Work to the corner, taking the needle down through the fabric at 14.
- The turning stitch cannot finish and start with the same stitch, but you need to work from the same hole. Take the needle and come up at 15 (two threads up and two threads to the left of 14).
- Take it to the back at 16 (the same hole as for 14), then up at 17 (the same hole as for 12), and the new row is ready to begin.
- Work the stitches in the new direction as before, taking the needle down at 18 and back up at 19 (the same hole as for 15).

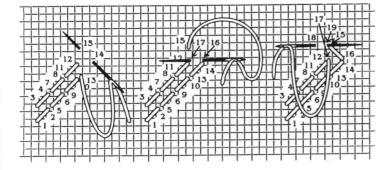

CUTTING AND WITHDRAWING THREADS

Good light and a pair of sharp, fine-pointed scissors are essential for cutting out. Never start cutting threads when you are tired. Cutting errors are hard to fix and very time-consuming, so it is better if they can be avoided.

All kloster blocks must be completed before cutting can begin. Each kloster block must have an opposite kloster block so that all ends are secured.

Each kloster block has a stitched edge and an unstitched edge. It is only along the satin-stitched edge that cutting takes place. Although there are five satin stitches, only the four fabric threads within the kloster block are actually cut.

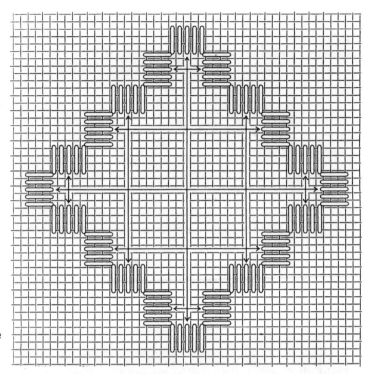

Arrows indicate
where you cut

All cutting is done from the back. The scissors are placed under the four threads with the scissor blade to the left of each kloster block. This makes the scissor blade as close as possible to the kloster block when cutting, eliminating fluffy cut threads.

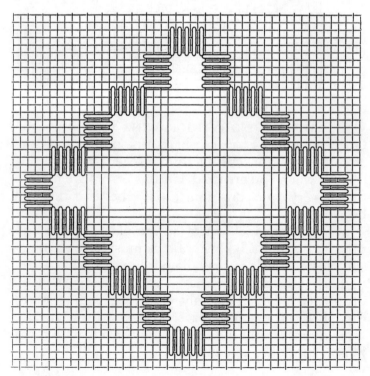

Grid of threads
with cut threads
withdrawn ready
for needleweaving

Place the blade under each thread, pull it up slightly and then cut the thread. **Only cut four threads on each block.** When the threads have been cut, carefully withdraw them (pull them out). A grid of threads as shown in the diagram should be left. These threads are now ready for needleweaving.

FIXING CUTTING MISTAKES
Mistakes can happen when cutting. If you cut incorrectly, do not panic. Mistakes can be fixed but it takes time and lots of patience. Here are some common problems and how you can deal with them

Five threads have been cut instead of only four threads at one end of a kloster block

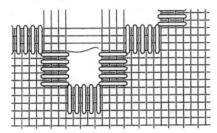

Withdraw the surrounding threads as usual. There will be a bar with four threads at one end and three threads plus the cut thread at the other end. Starting at the end with the four threads, needleweave as usual, making sure that the loose thread is caught securely at the other end. This woven bar may not be quite as wide as other woven bars.

The unsewn edge of the kloster block is cut
Withdraw the cut threads back to the edge of the embroidery. Carefully withdraw the same number of threads from the edge of the fabric. Weave these threads back into the fabric where the cut threads were withdrawn. Repeat this process ending each thread inside the kloster block, until each of the withdrawn threads have been replaced.

The kloster block thread or buttonhole edging thread is cut while cutting the fabric threads
Very carefully undo several kloster blocks on both sides of the cut block until there is enough thread to secure an end. Secure the threads at both ends. With a new thread, restitch the kloster blocks making sure the thread is not pulled too tight. Secure both ends of the new thread.

For the buttonhole edging, undo enough of the thread in both directions to secure the ends. With a new thread, restitch the buttonhole edging.

WOVEN BARS (NEEDLEWEAVING)

When threads have been cut and withdrawn, a grid of threads is left. These threads are then needlewoven. Needleweaving strengthens the cut threads and also adds decorative stitching to the finished embroidery. Needleweaving can be left plain, or other stitches such as picots, dove's eyes or square filets can be added. Each of these stitches is ornamental and adds to the lacy effect of the finished embroidery.

Woven bars are done with a coton perle no. 8 and no. 12.

- Starting with a waste knot, come up at 1.
- There should be four weft threads. Place the needle over the first two threads then take the needle under the third and fourth threads. Now reverse the process. Take the needle over the third and fourth threads, and then under the first two threads. A figure 8 has been made under and over the weft threads. Repeat this process until the bar has been filled: there will usually be seven stitches on both sides of each bar. Like the kloster blocks, the needleweaving is done in steps until all the bars are completed.

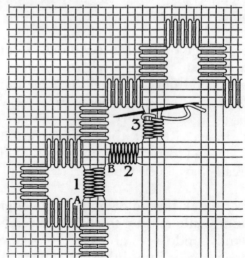

- To move from one bar to the next, the thread should be brought up from under the first bar to where the bars intersect (2). Take the needle and go over the first two threads of the next bar, then under the third and fourth threads. Continue the needleweaving until the bar is finished.

- When finishing the thread, take it to the back of the embroidery and run the thread through the stitching on one side of the woven bar and then through the second side of the bar. Going back to the beginning of the thread, cut the waste knot and finish the thread using the same method as above.

When using variegated thread, it is better to weave a square at a time instead of stepping the embroidery up the bars. Variegated thread can look quite messy if rows are embroidered.

Picots

Picots are combined with the needleweaving to add a lace effect to the embroidery. They are done with a coton perle no. 8 or no. 12.

Picots can be embroidered on both sides of each woven bar, or worked on one side of the bar in combination with another stitch.

PICOT TO THE RIGHT

- Needleweave half of the bar, finishing with the thread to the right of the bar.
- Take the needle and place it under the two threads on the right side of the bar with the needle pointing to the right again.
- Take the needle and place it under the two left threads with the needle pointing to the left.
- Take the thread under the needle and wrap it around once (like a French knot). Place your thumb over the thread to hold it in place.
- Pull the needle through carefully, leaving a small loop. Do not pull the loop tight or you will lose the picot. Continue needleweaving to complete the bar.

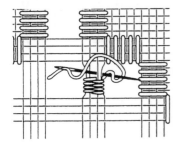 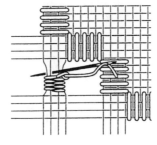

PICOT TO THE LEFT

- Weave half the bar, finishing on the left side of the bar.
- Take the thread under the needle, and wrap it around the needle once. Place your thumb over the thread and needle to hold it in place.
- Pull the needle through in the same way as a picot to the right. Continue needleweaving to complete the bar.

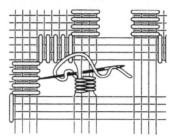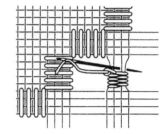

DOVE'S EYES

Dove's eyes are another decorative stitch used in combination with woven bars. They are stitched at the same time as the needleweaving is being done. They are worked in coton perle no. 8 or no. 12. All the loops should cross over in the same direction.

- Needleweave 3½ sides of the square.
- Coming up underneath the bar, finish with the needle in the centre of the square.
- Take the needle, place it through the middle of the previous bar and bring it up in the centre of the square, looping the thread under the needle.

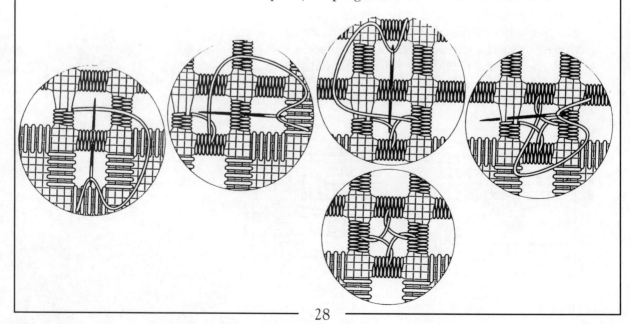

- Repeat this process until three sides have been completed.
- Take the needle and place it under the very first loop, then take it over the first two threads of the last bar and continue the needleweaving until the bar is completed.

SQUARE FILETS

These stitches are similar to dove's eyes but are worked from corner to corner of the block. They are usually used in conjunction with woven bars and picots. All square filets should be worked around the square in either a clockwise or an anti-clockwise direction. They will cross differently if worked in a different direction.

- Needleweave all four sides of a square, placing picots on the outside of the bars.
- When the bars are completed, come up at A. There needs to be two fabric threads on each side of A.
- Find B (this will also have two fabric threads on each side) and come up from underneath.
- Take the needle and place it **under** the loop made by the thread from A to B. Pull the needle through.
- Take the needle and come up at C.
- Take the needle under the second loop and pull it through.
- Bring the needle up at D.
- Place the needle under the third loop and pull it through.
- Take the needle and place it over the first loop and take it through to the back. There is a small straight stitch on the back from the last woven bar to A. Slip the needle under this stitch and pull it through. The thread can now be taken to the next bar for needleweaving.

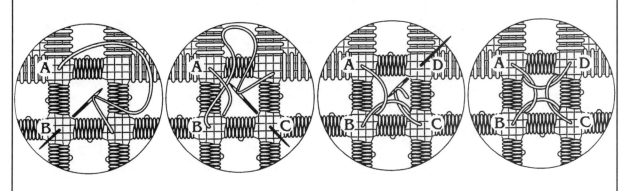

MALTESE CROSSES

This is a very decorative stitch. It gives a very lacy effect. It is done with the finer of the two threads, the coton perle no. 8 or no. 12.

- On the inside of each square block of 12 threads, cut four fabric threads from the corner, working in to the centre of the square. Withdraw these cut threads. There should be four threads in the centre of the square both vertically and horizontally. These are the threads the Maltese Cross will be worked on.
- To start, run the thread back and forth twice under the satin stitching on the back and come up at 1.
- Starting at 1, wrap the two threads on the right four times if using coton perle no. 8 and five times if using coton perle no. 12.
- With the next wrap, take the thread under the first two horizontal threads on the right. Now weave back and forth, over and under, between the two sets of threads, making eight stitches in all (four on each set of threads), ending at the two unwrapped threads.
- Wrap these threads four or five times, depending on the thread you are using. This completes the first quarter of the block.
- Repeat the process with the remaining bars.

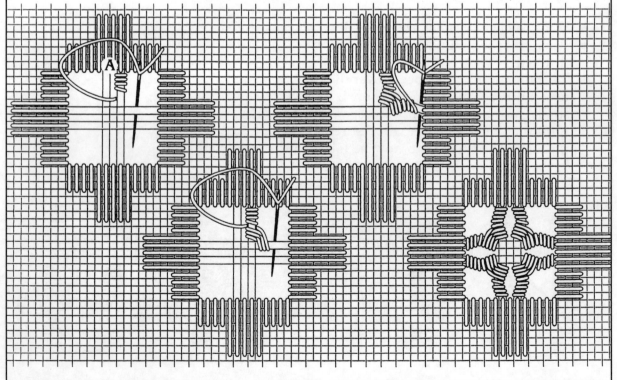

BUTTONHOLE STITCH

Buttonhole stitch is used around the edge of hardanger embroidery to give a secure edge. For each fabric thread, there is one buttonhole stitch along a straight edge. This varies when working around a corner.

The coarser thread — when working coton perle no. 5 or no. 8 — is used for buttonhole stitching. Whichever thread is used for the kloster blocks, is the same thread used for the buttonhole stitching. This stitch is worked from left to right.

There is a buttonhole stitch to correspond with every kloster block stitch, plus three corner stitches. On an inside corner, the last stitch of one group of buttonhole stitches and the first stitch of the next group share a hole with stitches of adjacent kloster blocks.

TURNING AN OUTSIDE CORNER

- Start buttonhole stitching eight threads below the corner of a kloster block. Starting with a waste knot, come up at A.
- Count four threads vertically up from A and one row to the right, place the needle in at B and back out at C, one thread to the right of A.
- Loop the thread under the needle and pull the needle through. This is the first stitch.
- Make three more stitches in exactly the same way.
- To turn the outside corner, the thread is pivoted at B, while counting two threads to the right of the last stitch and coming up at C.
- The thread is again pivoted at B and, counting two threads to the right, the needle comes up at D.
- Now turn the fabric around 90° so the buttonhole stitching that you have just completed is placed vertically over the fingers of your left hand.
- Put the needle in to the fabric at B again, count two threads to the right of D and come up at E.

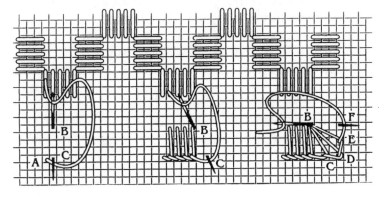

- The final stitch is made by going into the fabric at B, counting over two more threads to the right of E and coming up at F. The corner has now been turned. The last stitch made is the first of the five buttonhole stitches that run parallel with the kloster block immediately above it.

TURNING AN INSIDE CORNER

- Work an outside corner and the five buttonhole stitches to correspond with the kloster block.
- Count up four threads and slip the needle in, coming up in the same hole as the last buttonhole stitch.
- Loop the thread under the needle and pull it through.
- Make another four buttonhole stitches. This completes the inside turn.

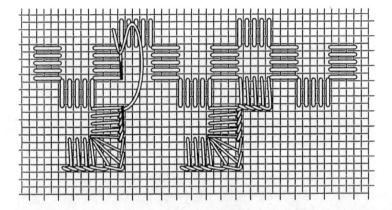

STARTING AND FINISHING A THREAD
Initially a waste knot is used on the end of the thread. After the thread has been used, the end is run under the previous stitching. Cut the waste knot off and run the end under the stitching.

CUTTING AROUND BUTTONHOLE STITCHING
All embroidery must be completed before cutting around the outside edges takes place.

Hardanger embroidery is cut out from the back. Place the blade of the scissors under the fabric threads as close to the buttonhole stitching as possible. Lift each thread and carefully cut it. Continue around the complete design. This is the most time-consuming part of the embroidery. Care must be taken so that the buttonhole stitching is not cut as well as the fabric threads.

HOLBEIN STITCH

This is a running stitch worked over two threads each time. The first row partially outlines the shape and the stitching is then reversed and the spaces filled in.

- Following the diagram, make stitches 1, 2, 3 and 4.
- Now reverse the direction, and complete the line by embroidering stitches 5, 6, 7 and 8. When embroidering the second line of stitches, come out at the right of 4 and go down to the left of 3. Repeat this process so a continuous line is formed.

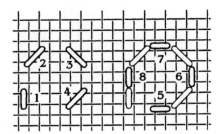

ROSETTE

I have used this stitch extensively for the Flannel Flower doily and also for some of the other projects. The needleweaving is surrounded by a satin stitch square. There must be 12 x 12 fabric threads within the square.

- Cut four fabric threads starting from each corner and working towards the centre. Withdraw the

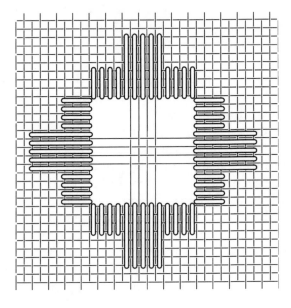

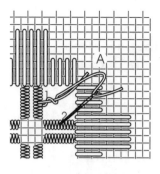
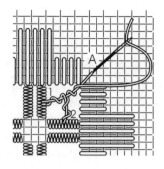

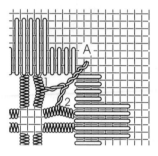

threads. There should be a cross of four fabric threads horizontally and four vertically in the centre of the square.

- The needleweaving is usually embroidered using the finer of the two threads used for each project. Each set of instructions will give the required thread to use.

- Thread the tapestry needle. Anchor the thread by weaving it under one side of the square and half way back to the centre where the intact fabric threads are. Come to the front of the fabric between threads 2 and 3.

- Starting with the fabric threads on bar 1, needleweave fabric threads one and two in a figure 8 until the bar in completely filled. Continuing on bar 2, needleweave the whole bar, ending with the needle at the back of the embroidery.

- Run the needle through the satin stitching on the back to the corner at A. Bring the needle through from the back at A to the front of the fabric where the fabric threads intersect in a square from the satin stitching. Take the needle and push it through the bar halfway between the satin stitching and bar 2. Push the needle through to the back and then wrap the thread twice. Pull gently and firmly to pull the bar slightly out of shape.

- Repeat this process on bar 2 until the wrapped thread is an inverted V shape. Wrap the thread leading to the corner at A twice and complete the stitch by going back into A from the top of the fabric.
- Run the needle through to the intersection of completed bar two and incomplete bar 3.
- Repeat the above instructions on the remaining bars.

BLANKET STITCH FLOWER

This stitch is very effective in replicating a flower and I have used it on many projects.

The cut work square must be enclosed by the satin stitching and have 20 x 20 fabric threads within the square. There are three sets of threads cut, four in each corner and four in the centre and then withdrawn. All the bars are woven then the flower is woven over the top of them.

- Anchor the thread with a waste knot and then come to the front of the fabric at the intersection of the horizontal and vertical bars in the top right corner as shown on the diagram. Take the needle and thread over the horizontal bar and complete a blanket (buttonhole) stitch on the vertical bar. Repeat the blanket stitch on the vertical bar. Take the thread back under horizontal bar to end in the centre square again.

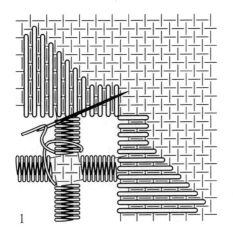

1

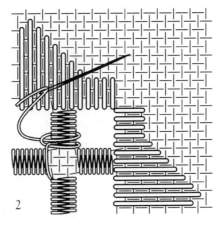

2

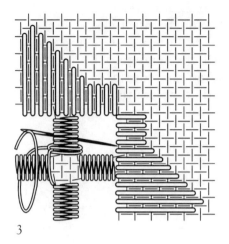

3

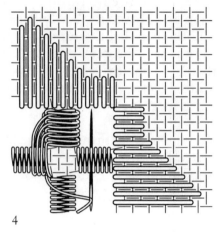

4

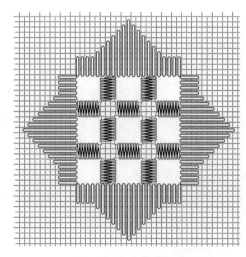

5

6

- Repeat this process until the vertical bar is filled and the needleweaving underneath cannot be seen.
- Take the needle and pass it under the needleweaving on the vertical bar and then the horizontal bar to end at the intersection of bars in the top left corner.
- Repeat the above process until all the stitching has been completed. It has to be done eight times to complete the flower.
- Cut the waste knot, thread the needle and run the thread under the closest bar. The centre of the flower can be left without any embroidery or a

square filet may be embroidered. Follow instructions for embroidering a square filet stitch in this chapter.

DIVIDED WRAPPED BARS

These squares have a very lacy effect and have been used on the Shades of Green doily. There must be a satin stitched square which encloses 12 x 12 fabric threads. Four threads from each corner are cut and withdrawn.

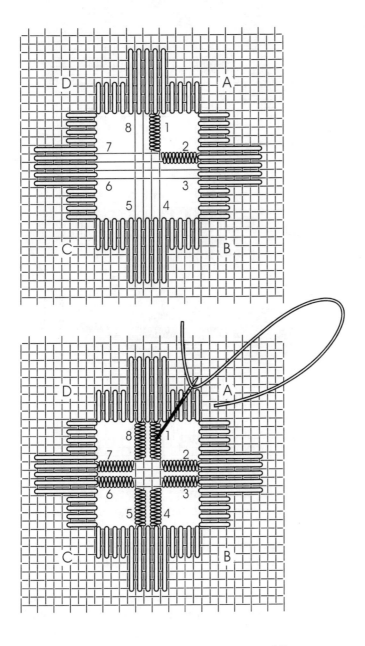

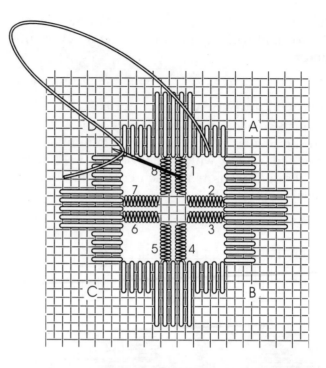

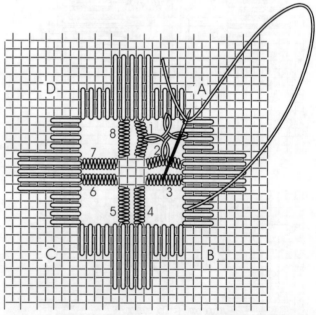

- Anchor the thread under the satin stitching on the back and come to the front between fabric threads 2 and 3.
- Wrap the fabric threads on bars 1 and 2. Repeat this process on bars 3 and 4, 5 and 6 and then bars 7 and 8.
- Starting at A, bring the needle to the front on the third satin stitch from the corner and embroider a

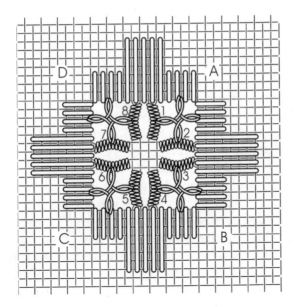

Dove's Eye using the two satin stitched edges and bars 1 and 2. Pull the thread gently to pull the bars into a curve.

- Run the needle under the satin stitching to the next corner and repeat the process. Repeat this process until all four corners have been embroidered.
- A bead may be attached in the centre or it can be left without any adornment.

HERRINGBONE STITCH

I have used herrringbone stitch on the Wedding Cushion. It is an effective border stitch. This stitch can be used for ordinary embroidery as well as a counted thread stitch. I used the Gumnut silk thread for this stitch.

- Anchor the thread with a waste knot and come through to the front at A. Counting four threads to the right and then four threads vertically down, go through to the back at B. Bring the needle to the front at C, four threads to the left of B, then back at D, four threads to the right of A. This sets the placement of the stitching.
- Now bring the needle to the front at E, two threads to the left of D, and then through to the back at F, two threads from B and then to G, then through to the back at H, two threads to the right of D. Repeat this process, remembering that there will be two threads sharing each hole, and that the stitches

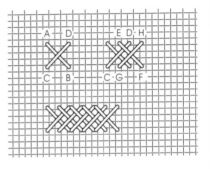

will be two threads apart horizontally and four threads vertically.

LACY EDGING

This edging is no harder than the ordinary buttonhole edging that I usually use to finish my hardanger embroidery. It is however, a little more delicate, but just as durable if treated properly.

To have the lacy edging it is necessary to have a row of kloster blocks along the outside edge of the embroidery. The fabric threads are cut along the satin stitched edge closest to the outside edge of the fabric, as if cutting for any other sort of needleweaving project. The fabric threads are cut and then withdrawn as normal. The finer of the two embroidery threads is used for the needleweaving and the final row of the edging. Start and finish all threads under the needleweaving of the closest bar. Any sort of needleweaving can be embroidered along this edge, using either plain needleweaving or including other stitches like Dove's Eyes or Square Filets.

- To complete the final edge, a combination of stitching is used. The bars are woven and the corner is turned using buttonhole stitch, as shown in

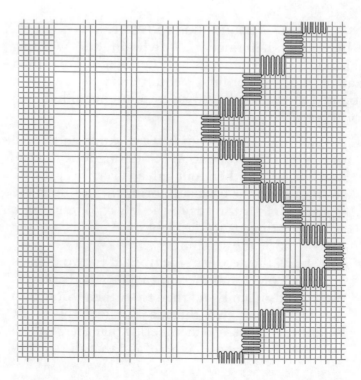

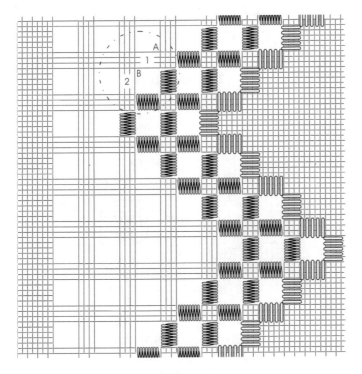

the diagram. Buttonhole stitches are made between each fabric thread on the corners.

- When the embroidery is complete along the outside edge, turn over to the back. Using a sharp pair of scissors, cut the fabric threads behind the buttonhole stitching. Be careful not to pull the stitching as it will pull off the bars and ruin the embroidery.

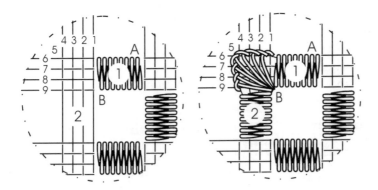

DECORATIONS AND DECORATIVE EMBROIDERY

BACK STITCH

Back stitch is a stitch used for outlining highlighting or to define a straight line. The stitch is worked from right to left.

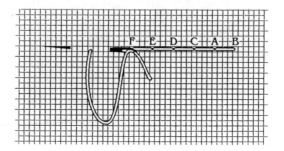

- Using a waste knot, go through the fabric from the top 8 cm (3 in) from A. Come up at A.
- Take the needle and place into B (four threads to the right of A) and bring the needle to the front.
- Take the needle back at A and then jump to C (four threads to the left of A). The needle and thread are always ahead of the stitch to be made, and you go back to the previous stitch to complete it.
- To end the thread, run it under the stitching on the back. Cut the waste knot from the beginning of the thread and repeat the process to finish it.

BULLION STITCH

- Using a waste knot, come up at A.
- With the needle facing towards you, take a straight stitch four fabric threads away at B. Pull the needle and thread completely through.

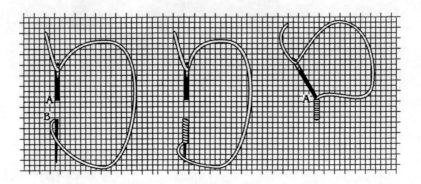

- Take the needle back to A and come up at B again, but do not pull the needle through.
- Take the thread and wrap it around the needle nine times.
- Using your thumbnail, push the wraps down the needle towards the fabric. Place your thumb on the wraps and pull the needle through. Pull the needle away from you so that the thread is tight. This should make the wraps sit against the fabric.
- Take the needle down through A again. The stitch is now complete.
- The ends of the thread are run through the stitching on the back to finish off.

Colonial knots

This knot is used as the centre of daisies, whether they are worked in bullion or lazy daisy stitch.

- To start the thread, run it under the stitches surrounding the point where the colonial knot is to be placed.
- Place the fabric on a hard surface. With your left hand, hold the thread approximately 5 cm (2 in) from A, with your thumb and first finger.
- Take the needle in your right hand and move the needle under the thread from the left side. Take the thread in your left hand and place it over the top of the needle, then under the right side of the needle.
- Place the needle back in the fabric one thread to the right of A.

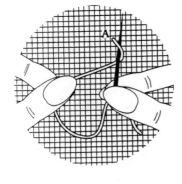
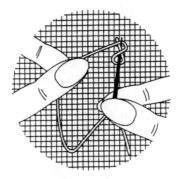

- Before taking the needle through to the back, pull the knot tight and then pull it through. The knot is now completed. If the knot is not pulled up tight, the stitch will be large and loopy. The thread makes a figure of eight around the needle.
- Finish the thread by running it under the stitching surrounding the colonial knot.

LAZY DAISY STITCH

- Coming up at A, take the needle back into A and come up at B (four fabric threads from A).
- Before pulling the needle through, take the thread and loop it under the needle. Pull the needle through carefully, leaving enough thread to make a fat petal or leaf.
- Take the needle and push it through to the back close to B, on the outside of the loop. This secures the loop and allows you to start the next daisy stitch.
- The straight stitch inside the loop is made from A to B.

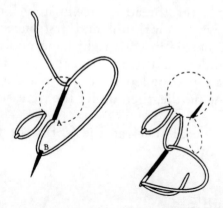

BULLION LAZY DAISY STITCH IN RIBBON

This is a variation on the standard lazy daisy stitch. A small bullion stitch takes the place of the usual anchor stitch at the point of the stitch. The shape of the petal or leaf will depend on the length of the bullion stitch used and the anchor point of the bullion.

The secret of this stitch is to keep the ribbon taut at all times and not to be afraid to tighten it firmly before anchoring the bullion.

- Bring the needle up at 1, down at 2 (just to the right of 1) and out again at 3, remembering that the bullion part of the stitch will extend beyond this point. Care should be taken to keep the ribbon flat at all times.

- Holding the ribbon firmly against the needle between points 1 and 3, fold the ribbon at right angles as it is passed under the needle at 3.
- Wrap it around the point of the needle two or three times, keeping it smooth and flat and spiraling the wraps up the needle so that they do not overlap too much.
- Lay the ribbon firmly to the base of the petal and hold it in place by covering with the left thumb as you pull the needle through, keeping the ribbon close to the fabric and in line with the bullion stitch. Try to tighten the stitch firmly by 'stretching' the stitch away from the base of the petal, not by pushing the stitch down towards the base of the petal with the left thumb.
- Pull the bullion tip 'off line' to create in the selected position a more natural appearance, and anchor by passing the needle to the back of the work at the tip of the petal.

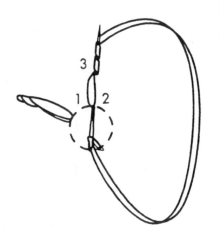

DETACHED BUTTONHOLE OR CAST-ON STITCH

Secure the thread with a small back stitch where it will be hidden under the flower centre.

- Bring the needle up through the fabric at point 1.
- Take a back stitch going down at 2 and back out at 1, taking care not to pierce the thread at point 1 or to pull the needle right through the fabric.
- Slip the first finger of your right hand into the thread loop (diag. 1).
- Hold the thread over the thumb nail and across the middle finger of the right hand to tension the thread as you twist the loop and slide it into the needle (diag. 2).
- Pull the thread until the loop tightens around the needle, making sure the loop slides to fit snugly at the point where the needle emerges through the fabric (diag. 3). (The knot created is a half hitch.)
- Repeat until the required number of loops have been worked onto the needle, making sure that each one fits snugly beside the previous one. There should be no gaps and no overlapping loops (diag. 4).
- Pull the needle through the fabric gently holding the loops between the finger and thumb of the left

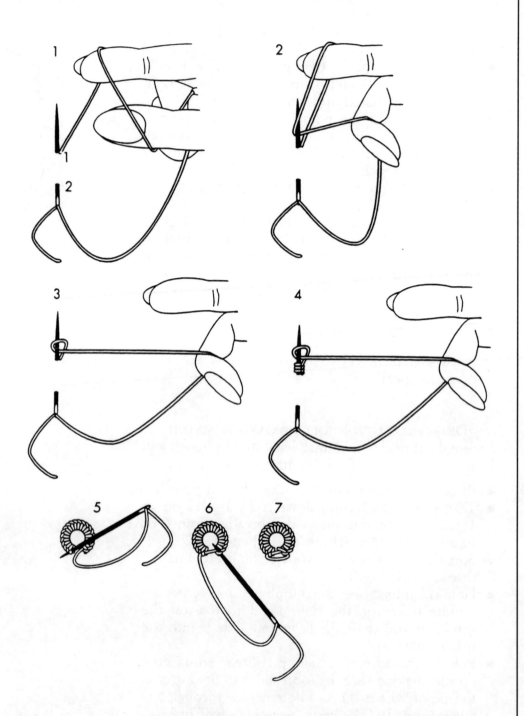

hand. Tighten the thread until the loops fill the length of the core thread.

- Anchor the stitch by passing the needle to the back of the work at point 2. For loop stitches, used for petals, 1 and 2 are close together. To form the stitch into a cup shape, pull the base of the stitch in closer by stitching together the first and last knot, as shown in diagrams 5, 6 and 7.

FLY STITCH

- Bring the needle up at 1, then down at 2 and out again at 3. Keep the thread from point 1 looped under the needle at 3 and pull the needle through (diag 1).
- Anchor the stitch by passing the needle through to the back of the work at 4 (diag. 2). Note that a small stalk can be created by moving point 4 further away from 3.

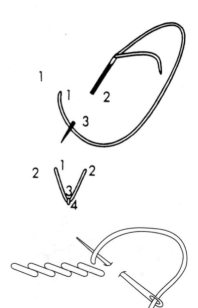

STEM STITCH

- Bring the needle out at 1, down at 2 and out again at 3 (where 3 is halfway between 1 and 2) with the ribbon below the needle (diag 1).
- Keeping the ribbon below the needle, take the needle down at 4 and back out at 5 (diag. 2).

MAKING A TASSEL

- Cut 2 m (1½ yd) length of thread.
- Cut a 6.5 cm (2½ in) square of cardboard.
- Thread a tapestry needle with a 20 cm (8 in) length of matching thread. Slip the needle under one end of the wrapped thread and tie it in a knot.
- Remove the cardboard from the thread. Take another piece of thread 20 cm (8 in) long and wrap it around the tassel head 1 cm (½ in) from the tied end. Finish the end of the thread by running it under some of the wraps.
- Thread a tapestry needle with a length of matching thread 20 cm (8 in) long and embroider a row of buttonhole stitching around the wraps and end the thread.

- Cut the looped ends and trim them to look neat, if necessary. Use the tied piece of thread to attach the tassel.

EMBROIDERED FLOWERS

I have added these flowers to projects. They are embroidered on after the other work is completed.

FLANNEL FLOWERS

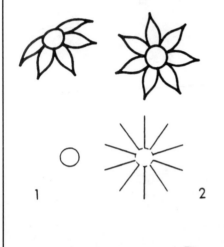

- Draw a circle about 6 mm (¼ in) in diameter.
- Work 9 to 11 bullion lazy daisy petals, each between 9 mm and 11 mm (⅜ in and ½ in) total length, around the centre. Wrap the ribbon two or three times for each bullion.

Note: A more natural shape will be achieved if some of the stitches are slightly off-line. To create a smooth stitch, make sure the ribbon is laid flat at all times and spiralled up the needle when working the bullion wraps. Hold the stitch firmly under the thumb as the needle is pulled through the fabric, and tighten the ribbon by pulling firmly on the ribbon while keeping it close to the fabric. Do not push wraps down with the thumb.

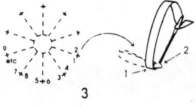

- Fill the centre with colonial knots in green.
- Using green, work a back stitch over the tip of each petal. Bring the needle up through the fabric under the tip, wrap the ribbon neatly around the tip, and return the needle to the back of the work through the same hole. (Slipping a spare needle under the ribbon as the stitch is tightened will ensure the ribbon lies flat over the bullion.)

ROSES

- Work a 10-wrap detached buttonhole stitch picking up two or three threads of the fabric for the base stitch (diag 1).
- Pull the base of the stitch close by stitching together with a tiny straight stitch before passing the needle to the back of the work between the anchor points.
- Work four 12-wrap overlapping stitches around the centre stitch (diag 2).
- Change to a paler shade of thread and work a circle of six 12-wrap overlapping stitches around the outer edge of the first circle (diag 3).

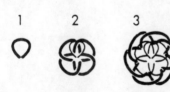

DAISIES

- Mark a small circle for the centre, approximately 2 mm (1/16 in) in diameter (diag 1).
- Stitches are about 7 mm (just over 1/4 in) in length with 12 wraps.
- Work four stitches starting at the outer edge of the marked circle at 12, 3, 6 and 9 o'clock (diag 2).
- Fill each gap with three stitches to complete the daisy (diag 3).
- Fill the centre with colonial knots worked with one strand of Flower Thread or two of stranded cotton.

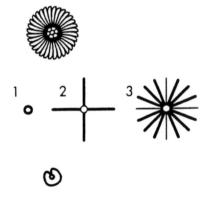

To create a small daisy, use a finer thread and start with a smaller centre (a single dot). Work the marker stitches, about 5 mm (3/16 in) long and 10 wraps, and finish with a single colonial knot for the centre.

SWEET PEAS

- Work two detached buttonhole stitches with 8 wraps for the centre. Stitch these two stitches together at both ends to make them stand up (diag 1).
- Work a 24-wrap stitch around the first two stitches, taking care not to pull the stitch too tight (diag 2).
- Work a stitch of 32 wraps around the edge of the previous stitches, adjusting the tension carefully so that the stitches just overlap.
- Stitch the last two stitches down on the fabric at the centre top of the flower (diag 3).
- Shape the base of the flower by pulling the petals together towards the centre with a tiny holding stitch.

CHAPTER 3
PROJECTS

Kloster Blocks

Eyelet

Satin Stitch

Cable Stitch

Colonial Knot

Bead

Buttonhole Edging

Lacy Edging

Holbein Stitch

Needleweaving

Doves Eye

Square Filet

Rosette

Divided Wrapped Bars

Maltese Cross

Blanket Stitch Flower

PINCUSHIONS

BLACK CURRANT PINCUSHION

REQUIREMENTS
1 x 19 cm (7½ in) square of 28 count cream fabric
1 skein Gumnut Yarns Buds no. 198 or DMC coton
  perle no. 8 wine
1 skein Gumnut Yarns Buds no. 584 or DMC stranded cotton pale green
1 card Petals Silk Ribbon Black Currant, 7 mm silk
  ribbon wine
1 tapestry needle no. 24
1 tapestry needle no. 18
1 Ireland Needlecraft pincushion with wooden base
1 small spring hoop

METHOD
The size of the fabric may seem enormous for such a
small amount of embroidery in the centre, but it is
necessary because the fabric needs to be gathered
around the pincushion.

- Starting in the centre of the fabric, count out two threads in any direction. This is the starting point for the embroidery.
- Using tapestry needle no. 24 and a length of the no. 198 silk thread, satin stitch the flower motifs in the centre of the fabric.
- When this is completed, mark the centre of each flower placement with a water erasable pen or pencil.
- Using the hoop, a short length of silk ribbon and tapestry needle no. 18, embroider each silk ribbon flower around the marked centres using a twisted chain stitch.
- Changing to a length of Buds silk thread no. 584 and tapestry needle no. 24, embroider a single colonial knot in the centre of the satin stitched motif and six colonial knots in the centre of each silk ribbon flower, one in the centre and five surrounding it.

When all embroidery is complete, draw a pencil line circle around the embroidery which has a 19 cm (7½ in) diameter. Cut the fabric along this line. Using a strong quilting thread doubled, run a tacking or basting thread around the outside edge of the circle 7 mm (⅜ in) from the edge of the fabric, leaving a thread end of approximately 7.5 cm (3 in) at each end.

The pincushion top is screwed to the wooden base. Unscrew this and put the screw aside. Place the embroidery on a hard surface face down. Place the pincushion top on the embroidery with the screw hole facing you. Pull the tacking or basting threads at each end until the fabric is pulled tightly around the pincushion top. Tie a knot in the thread several times making sure it does not become loose. You may have to 'borrow' someone's finger for this. Make sure the thread is tight. Using your finger, carefully move the gathers until they are evenly distributed around the pincushion top. Turning the pincushion top upside down, trim any excess fabric. Place the wooden base on over the top and screw the two together. Turn up the right way.

MAUVE DELIGHT PINCUSHION

REQUIREMENTS

2 x 13 cm (5 in) square of cream Jubilee
1 skein Gumnut Silk Buds no. 299 or DMC coton
  perle no. 8 dark mauve
1 skein Gumnut Silk Buds no. 297 or DMC coton
  perle no. 8 light mauve
1 x tapestry needle no. 24
1 x 13 cm (5 in) square of coloured fabric
toy stuffing

METHOD
Centre

- Using the tapestry needle and Buds no. 297, follow
  the graph for the centre embroidery of the pincushion and embroider the squares using satin
  stitch.
- Change to Buds no. 299 and embroider the straight
  stitches in the centre of the four corners and the

centre satin stitched squares.

- Cut and withdraw the threads from the other four squares and embroider Maltese Crosses using Buds no. 299.

Border

There are three rows of satin stitching which create a border around the embroidery in the centre. Using Buds no. 297 and tapestry no. 24 needle, embroider the row closest to the centre and the outside row using satin stitch. Change to Buds no. 299 and satin stitch the inner row of the border.

When all embroidery has been completed, place the coloured piece of fabric under the embroidery and machine sew the two pieces together. With right sides together, sew the second piece of Jubilee to the front on three sides and just past the corners on the fourth side. Clip the corners and turn right side out. Press gently with an iron and push the corners out to be square.

Stuff the pincushion with toy stuffing. Pin the fourth edge together and using a needle and thread, slip stitch together. Gently manipulate the filling to be evenly distributed in the pincushion.

BLUE DAISY PINCUSHION

REQUIREMENTS

2 x 15cm (6 in) square of cream Jubilee
1 skein Gumnut Yarns Buds no. 389 or DMC coton perle no. 8 sky blue
1 card Wisteria Silk Ribbon or 4 mm mauve or sky blue ribbon
1 packet of Mill Hill Beads no. 00252 mauve/blue
1 tapestry needle no. 24
1 tapestry needle no. 18
1 beading needle
cream quilting thread
toy stuffing

METHOD

- Using tapestry needle no. 24 and Buds silk thread no. 389, start in the centre of the fabric and embroider all the kloster blocks.
- When the kloster blocks are completed, mark where the centre of each flower is to be placed on

the fabric with a water erasable pen.

- Using a short length of Petals Wisteria silk ribbon and tapestry needle no. 18, embroider the daisies with five or six petals on each flower using a lazy daisy stitch.
- Changing to the beading needle and a matching cream thread, attach three Mill Hill beads in the centre of each flower using a half cross stitch for each bead. Attach a bead in the centre of each of the four diamonds in the centre of the pattern.

When all embroidery has been completed, make up pincushion. With right sides facing together, sew along three edges of the pincushion and just past the corners on the fourth side. Clip the corners and then turn right side out. Press gently with an iron and push the corners out to be square. Stuff with the toy stuff-

ing. Pin the edges together along the opening and slip stitch together with needle and matching thread.

Using the beading needle and matching quilting thread, pick up four beads at a time and using a straight stitch, attach a row of beads around the edge of the pincushion. They will tuck in nicely along the seam edge. When this is completed, manipulate the stuffing to fill all the corners of the pincushion.

RAYS OF GOLD PINCUSHION

REQUIREMENTS

2 x 12.5 cm (5 in) squares cream Jubilee
1 skein Gumnut Yarns Buds no. 745 or DMC coton
    perle no. 8 light yellow
1 skein Gumnut Yarns Buds no. 746 or DMC coton

perle no. 8 dark yellow
1 packet of Mill Hill Beads no. 00557, gold
1 tapestry needle no. 24
1 beading needle
1 coloured piece of fabric 12.5 cm (5 in) square
cream quilting thread
toy stuffing

METHOD

- Using the tapestry needle no. 24 and Buds no. 745, follow the graph and embroider the satin stitched square for the centre blanket stitch flower.
- Using the same coloured thread, embroider the kloster blocks, the back stitching and then the colonial knots.
- Cut the appropriate threads and then needleweave the bars of the centre square with Buds no. 745.
- Change to Buds no. 746 and embroider the blanket stitch flower over the bars and then the square filet in the centre of the flower.
- For the corners, embroider the kloster blocks with Buds no. 746, then cut and withdraw the appropriate threads. Following the graph, needleweave the bars with Buds no. 746, placing the square filet in the centre of each corner.
- Attach one bead in the centre of each kloster block square using the beading needle and a matching thread with half a cross stitch.

When all the embroidery is complete, pin the coloured piece of fabric under the embroidery and machine sew the two pieces together. With right sides together, sew the second piece of Jubilee to the front on three sides and just past the edges on the fourth side. Clip the corners and turn right side out. Press gently with the iron and push the corners out to be square. Stuff the pincushion with the toy stuffing. Pin the fourth edge together and using a needle and thread, slip stitch them together.

Using the beading needle and matching quilting thread, pick up four beads at a time and, using a straight stitch attach the beads around the edge of the pincushion. They will tuck in nicely along the seam edge. When this is completed, manipulate the stuffing to fill all the corners of the pincushion.

TILE PINCUSHION

REQUIREMENTS

2 x 20.5 cm (8 in) square of cream Jubilee
1 skein Gumnut Yarns Buds no. 547 or DMC coton
    perle no. 8 medium green
1 skein Gumnut Yarns Buds no. 543 or DMC coton
    perle no. 8 light green
1 tapestry needle no. 24
toy stuffing

METHOD

This pattern is worked on the diagonal of the fabric so it requires a fairly large piece of fabric.

- Starting in the centre, embroider the kloster blocks using the tapestry needle and Buds no. 547.
- Change to Buds no. 543 and embroider eyelets in the centre of the kloster blocks as shown on the graph.
- Still using Buds no. 543, embroider the row of cable stitch and the row of back stitching to create the square and diamond.
- Change to Buds no. 547 and embroider the inner four sets of triangles using satin stitching.
- Change to Buds no. 543 and embroider the outer two rows of cable stitching and then embroider the four sets of triangles with Buds no. 547.

When all the embroidery is complete, place the two pieces of Jubilee right sides together and machine sew them together along three sides and just past the corners on the fourth side. Clip the corners and turn right side out. Press gently with an iron and push the corners out to be square. Stuff with the toy stuffing. Pin the edges together along the opening and slip stitch together. Manipulate the stuffing around so it is evenly distributed in the pincushion.

SHAWL

I have embroidered this shawl using the Gumnut Yarns Gemstones wools. The wool is slightly variegated and I have used two shades of each colour. I have used two types of metallic thread, DMC for the eyelets and Madeira for the borders. Each metallic thread has a specific purpose and it is much easier to use the correct thread for their given tasks.

The panel of Ann cloth is a rectangle so there are seven embroidered motifs along the long side and five motifs on the shorter side. The cloth I used has two rows of pattern woven twice along all four edges. It is between the third and fourth rows that I embroidered the border design. I had to use two strands of each colour of wool to make sure there was good coverage over the fabric.

REQUIREMENTS

1 panel of Ann cloth, 118 cm x 140 cm (47 in x 55 in)
8 skeins each Gumnut Yarns Gemstones GL5 dark dusty pink, S4 dark mauve, TQ5 dark blue and D5 dark green
6 skeins each Gumnut Yarns Gemstones GL4 light dusty pink, S3 light mauve, TQ4 light blue and D3 light green
1 spool DMC Light Silver thread
1 spool Madeira Glamour silver no. 2442
1 tapestry needle no. 22

Graph A is the design for the four corners of the border.

Graph B is the border.

Graph C is the design for the centre of the cloth.

METHOD

- Start with the four corners of the border. Thread the tapestry needle with two strands of D5. Find the centre of each square and following graph A, embroider the central motif.
- Change to two strands of D3 and embroider the corner motifs.
- Change to a single strand of DMC silver thread and embroider the eyelets in the centre motif and in the four corners as shown on the graph. There are three fabric threads in between each motif

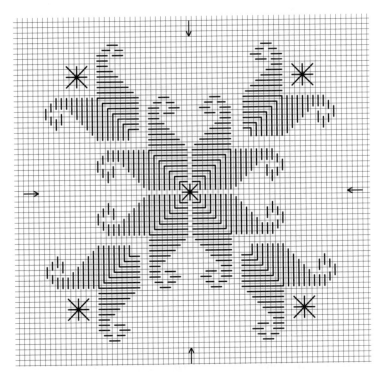

Graph A

Graph B

along the borders. The darkest shade of each wool is used to border the central motif on graph B.

• For the borders, find the centre of the longest side. This is the starting point. Thread the tapestry needle with two strands of GL5, and embroider the border of the motif.

Graph C

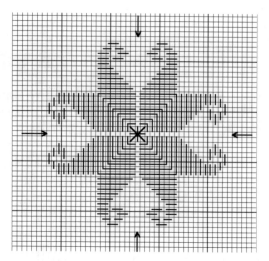

- Change to two strands of GL3 and embroider the central motif.
- Change to one strand of DMC silver thread and embroider an eyelet in the centre of the motif and the four corners as shown on the graph.
- Repeating these instructions, embroider the border working out from the centre to the corners. The colour selection I used, starting from the centre working towards the corners, is garnet, green, blue and then mauve as shown in the photograph.

For the shorter sides of the border, follow the above embroidery instructions. Start in the centre with the green and work out to the corners with the blue and then the mauve.

- For the centre motifs, find the centre of the inside rectangle of the Ann cloth. Using two strands of GL3 embroider the motif on graph C.
- Using one strand of DMC silver, embroider an eyelet in the centre of motif.
- Run a tacking or basting thread towards the middle of the shawl from the centre of the two blue motifs on the border until they intersect. Repeat this on the other three corners. This is the placement of the remaining motifs for the centre rectangle. Embroider each of these with two strands of GL3 for the motif and one strand of silver thread for the eyelets. Repeat this for all the corners.
- Using one strand of the Madeira silver thread, weave two rows between the first and second rows of woven pattern following the weave of the fabric. Repeat this between the third and fourth rows as well. Repeat this until all four sides are completed.

- Fringe 5 cm (2 in) along the outside edge of each side. Using groups of two threads, tie an overhand knot with the threads. Push the knot as close to the fabric as possible. Repeat this along all four edges.

POINSETTIA TRINKET BOX

REQUIREMENTS

1 x 13 cm (5 in) square 28 count white Jubilee
1 ball no. 8 coton perle
1 spool DMC Fils gold thread
1 card of Petals Red Wine silk ribbon or 4 mm silk ribbon wine
1 packet ·Mill Hill Beads no. 00557, gold
1 tapestry needle no. 24
1 tapestry needle no. 18
1 beading needle
1 x 13 cm (5 in) square dark blue fabric
toy stuffing
white quilting thread

METHOD

- Using tapestry needle no. 24 and coton perle no. 8, follow the graph and embroider the two rows of kloster blocks.
- Before the needleweaving can be started, it is necessary to embroider the poinsettias. Mark the centres of the flowers with a water soluble pen. Using tapestry needle no. 18 and Red Wine silk ribbon, embroider the poinsettias using the twisted chain stitch as placed on the graph.
- The beads may be attached at this stage or left until the needleweaving is completed. Attach with white quilting thread and the beading needle using a half cross stitch. Attach as many beads as you like. I placed seven in the middle of the centre flower and six in the centre of the outside half flowers.
- Cut the fabric threads and needleweave the Dove's Eyes as shown on the graph using coton perle no. 8 and a length of gold thread together and tapestry needle no. 24.

With each trinket box, there should be a kit for the lid. There is a piece of cardboard, a piece of clear plastic, a piece of felt and the gold edging for the lid. Place the blue fabric underneath the embroidery and run a tacking or basting thread around the outside edge to hold both pieces of fabric together. Using the quilting thread, run a gathering thread around the outside edge of the fabric. Place a small piece of toy stuffing on the wrong side of the fabric and then place the round piece of cardboard on top. Gather the fabric, making sure the embroidery is centred. Tie off tightly. Trim any excess fabric.

Press this into the lid making sure the embroidery is centred correctly. Remove the backing from the felt and press carefully into the underside of the lid.

I did not use the clear piece of plastic supplied in the kit, which is normally placed over the embroidery. The beads in the centre of the poinsettias would make indentations in the plastic, ruining it and detracting from the finished article.

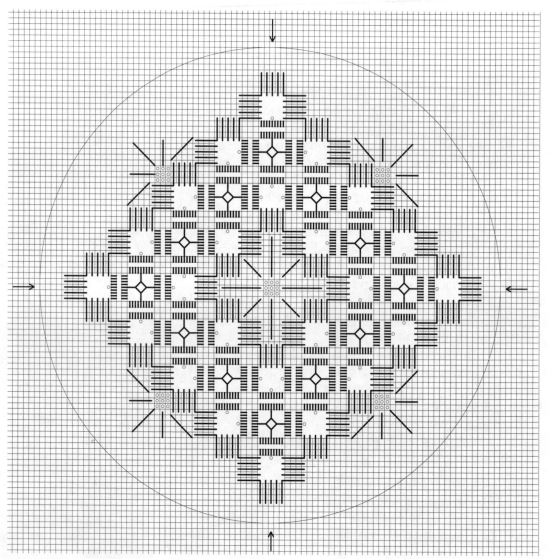

Pincushions — Black Currant (centre), Mauve Delight (top right), Blue Daisy (bottom left), Rays of Gold (top left), Tile (bottom right)

Above: Shawl
Left: Detail of Shawl

Poinsettia Trinket Box

Embroiderer's Box

Above: Shades of Green Doily
Below: Wedding Cushion and Detail of Wedding Cushion

EMBROIDERER'S BOX

My father made this box at my request for inclusion in this book. I felt sure that most people either knew someone who does woodwork or could ask a carpenter to make the box.

The dimensions are shown in diagram 1. The embroidery is 20 cm x 28 cm (8 in x 11 in) and is inserted into the lid of the box. I placed a piece of non reflective glass over the top of the embroidery to protect it from dust and wear. The embroidery was mounted on a piece of heavy coloured board and then clipped into the lid.

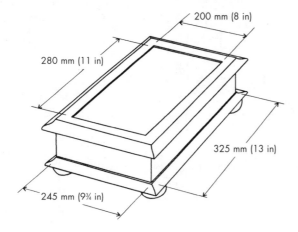

200 mm (8 in)

Diagram 1

280 mm (11 in)

325 mm (13 in)

245 mm (9¾ in)

REQUIREMENTS

1 piece of dusty pink Jobelan 30.5 cm x 40.5 cm (12 in x 16 in)
2 balls coton perle no. 8 no. 223, dark dusty pink
1 ball coton perle no. 8 no. 224, light dusty pink
1 tapestry needle no. 24

METHOD

- Starting in the centre of fabric and graph, use the tapestry needle and coton perle no. 223 and embroider the squares using holbein stitch. All of the squares can be embroidered as they are a continuous line to the edge.
- Continuing to use coton perle no. 223, embroider all the kloster blocks.
- Using coton perle no. 224, embroider a colonial knot in the centre of each set of kloster blocks.
- The small sets of four diamonds in the centre of

the holbein stitch blocks are embroidered using satin stitch and coton perle no. 224 with a colonial knot in the centre of each diamond using coton perle no. 223. The outside row of small diamonds is embroidered using coton perle no. 223.

- The blocks that have the blanket stitch flowers have all the bars woven first using coton perle no. 224. The flower is then embroidered using blanket stitch and coton perle no. 223 with a square filet in the centre of the flower.

- The blocks that have only the square filet in the centre have the outside row of bars woven using coton perle no. 224. The square filet is then embroidered using coton perle no. 223.

Repeat the pattern until the embroidery is complete.

SHADES OF GREEN DOILY

This doily has been embroidered using a lacy edging. It is as durable as the ordinary edging but needs a little more care. It will last as long as the hardanger embroidery with the buttonhole edging. It is also no more difficult than the buttonhole edging used in other projects and can be as wide as you like.

The needleweaving patterns that are used in any of the lacework parts of hardanger can be used for this edging.

I enjoyed this project tremendously when I embroidered it. I decided to be extrovert and added beads and green metallic thread to highlight various parts of the embroidery. If you don't like these additions, the doily can be embroidered without them.

REQUIREMENTS

1 piece of dark green Belfast linen 66 cm x 41 cm (26 in x 16 in)
2 balls ecru coton perle no. 8
2 balls ecru coton perle no. 12
2 packets Mill Hill beads no. 02020 dark green
1 spool Kreinik Balger Blending Filament no. 009 metallic dark green
1 tapestry needle no. 24
1 tapestry needle no. 26
1 beading needle
matching dark green quilting thread

METHOD

On the graph, I have marked A and B. This section is repeated on the doily six times but it is not necessary if you want to make a smaller doily. The graph also shows the corner.

The complete doily has four large diamonds of satin stitched squares along each side and three smaller diamonds along the centre.

- Starting in the centre of the fabric, use satin stitch and embroider the centre diamonds as shown on the graph using tapestry needle no. 24 and coton perle no. 8.
- Still using the same needle and thread, embroider the large diamond of satin stitching for the cutwork squares and the row that is within the row of squares. Then embroider the four diamonds in the centre.
- Continuing with the same needle and thread, embroider the stars, and then the row of kloster blocks around the outside edge.
- Changing to coton perle no. 12 and tapestry needle no. 26, embroider the eyelets inside each set of kloster blocks.
- Cut four fabric threads from each corner of the satin stitched squares and withdraw the threads.

Using coton perle no. 12 and the tapestry needle no. 26, embroider a divided wrapped bar in each square.

The Edging

- Following the row of kloster blocks along the edge, cut the threads on the outside closest to the edge of the fabric. Pull the fabric threads back towards the edge. It is necessary to withdraw at least 44 fabric threads.
- Using coton perle no. 12 and tapestry needle 26 embroider the edging as follows:
  Row 1. Needleweave all the bars.
  Rows 2,3 and 4. Needleweave 3 rows of Dove's Eyes.
  Row 5. This is the final edge. Needleweave the bars and buttonhole around each corner.
- Using Balger Filament thread and tapestry needle no. 24, back stitch around each segment of each star.
- Change to beading needle and the matching green thread and attach a bead in the centre of each star and each divided wrapped bar using a half cross stitch.
- Following the graph, attach beads where indicated on the three sets of diamonds along the centre of the doily. Attach three rows of beads as shown on the graph along the lacy edging.

Finally, it is necessary to cut the threads that attach the doily to the fabric. There are four threads horizontally and vertically on each corner that has been buttonhole stitched. Turn the doily to the back and cut each of these fabric threads very carefully. Do not pull the woven bars or the buttonhole stitching on each corner. Cut all the fabric threads. Press with an iron on the wrong side.

WEDDING CUSHION

REQUIREMENTS
For the embroidery

1 x 28 cm (11 in) square white Lugana
4 skeins Gumnut Yarns Silk Buds no. 584 green or
    DMC coton perle no. 8 ivory
1 skein Gumnut Yarns Silk Buds no. 584 green or
    DMC coton perle no. 8 pale green
1 skein Minnamurra stranded no. 40 pale pink or
    DMC stranded cotton pale pink
1 skein DMC no. 3052 dark green
1 spool Kanagawa metallic thread no. 403, green
1 packet 2 mm pearl beads
1 tapestry needle no. 24
1 beading needle
1 milliners no. 7

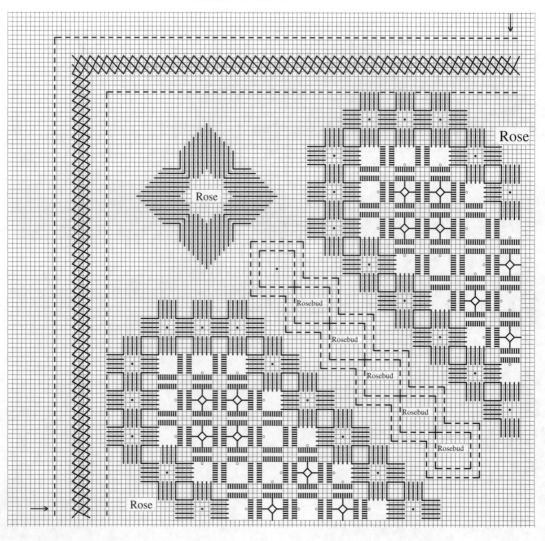

1 piece of 7 mm silk ribbon 36 cm (14 in) long
matching white quilting thread

For making the cushion

1 x 25 cm (10 in) square of ivory taffeta
2 x 14 cm x 25.5 cm (5½ in x 10 in) pieces of white
    Lugana
1 x 20 cm (8 in) white zipper
96 cm (38 in) cording for the edging
2 x 25 cm (10 in) pieces of ivory fabric, to make cush-
    ion insert
toy stuffing for cushion insert

METHOD

- Following the graph, start in the centre and count
  16 threads to the first kloster block.
- Using the Buds no. 991 and tapestry needle no. 24,
  embroider all the kloster blocks.
- Cut and withdraw the necessary threads within the
  heart.
- Still using the same needle and thread,
  needleweave the bars placing the Dove's Eyes and
  picots where shown on the graph.
- Using Buds no. 584, green, backstitch the intersect-
  ing squares on the diagonal in between the hearts
  and then satin stitch the four hearts in each corner.
- Using two strands of Minnamurra 40, pink and
  the milliners needle, embroider rosebuds on the
  diagonal of the five of the back stitched squares.
  For the centre of the rosebud, use 8 wraps on the
  needle for the bullion stitch.
- Change to two strands of DMC 3052 and one
  strand of the Kanagawa metallic thread, and
  embroider a bullion stitch on each side of the
  pink, using 10 wraps on the needle.
- With the same thread and needle, embroider a fly
  stitch around each rosebud with short stem pointing towards the corner of the square.
- Using Minnamurra 40 and the milliners needle,
  embroider the full blown rose in each corner set of
  hearts. The rose is embroidered using detached
  buttonhole stitch. The centre of the rose has 10
  wraps pulled up to make a circle, and the four outside petals have 12 wraps each. The rose leaves are
  embroidered using DMC 3052 and 10 wraps on
  the half closest to the rose and 12 wraps on the
  bottom of the petal.

- Embroider another rose in the top of each heart using the above instructions.
- Attach the 7 mm silk ribbon in the centre of the cushion using the bullion stitch rosebud described above.

The Border

- Back stitch the first row of the border as shown on the graph using Buds no. 584 and tapestry needle no. 24 .
- Change to Buds no. 991 and embroider the second row of the border using herringbone stitch.
- The third row is back stitched using Buds no. 584.
- Using the beading needle and matching white quilting thread, attach a pearl in the centre of each set of kloster blocks as shown on the graph. Also attach a pearl in the centre of the sixth back stitched green square.

When all the embroidery has been completed, take the two pieces of Lugana and press a hem 2 cm (¾ in) along the 25.5 cm (10 in) edge. Sew along the pressed line on the wrong side for 2 cm (¾ in) from each end. Pin the zipper along the unsewn seam between the sewn edges. Sew the zipper in.

The cord I bought had a flat piece which makes it much easier to attach it to the fabric. The first and last 5 cm (2 in) of the cord are pinned into one corner of the cushion. Pin the cording along the seam line on all four sides. Attach to the embroidered fabric on the seam line using a zipper foot. Undo the zipper. With right sides together, pin and then sew the two pieces together using the zipper foot. Trim across the corners and then turn right side out. Push the corners out to make them square. Steam press with an iron.

Sew the two pieces of ivory fabric together on three sides and past the corners on the fourth side. Stuff with the toy stuffing until it has reached the required fullness and then sew the two edges together.

Place the insert into the cushion. Manipulate the stuffing until it is evenly distributed throughout the cushion.

Flannel Flower Doily

Detail of Flannel Flower
Doily

Daisy Doily

Detail of Daisy Doily

Cards — Daisy (left), Rose (top), Sweet Pea (bottom right)

Christmas Decorations — 1 Blue Starburst, 2 Gold Flower Diamond, 3 Checked Diamond, 4 Starry Night, 5 Mosaic, 6 Bell, 7 Charm of Christmas, 8 Lacy Diamond, 9 Hearts of Christmas, 10 Emerald Starburst, 11 Star of Christmas, 12 Red Starburst

Flower Vest — front

Flower Vest — back

Roses of Autumn Doily

Detail of Roses of Autumn
Doily

Tulip Doily

Rose Heart and Delphinium Coaster

FLOWER DOILIES

These two doilies are both the same design but I have used different fabric and thread for each. I then added silk ribbon flannel flowers for one doily and bullion stitch daisies for the other. I did this to demonstrate the difference that colour, fabric and thread can make to an embroidered article.

FLANNEL FLOWER DOILY

REQUIREMENTS

1 x 41 cm (16 in) square of natural Jobelan
2 balls no. 8 coton perle no. 644 natural
8 metres of 2 mm cream silk ribbon
6 metres of 2 mm light green ribbon
1 tapestry needle no. 24
1 tapestry needle no. 18
1 skein Gumnut Yarn Buds no. 624 or DMC stranded cotton pale green

METHOD

- Starting in the centre of the fabric and graph, follow the graph and satin stitch the tulips using tapestry needle no. 24 and coton perle no. 8.
- Count 136 fabric threads from the centre, and then embroider the first row of cable stitch, the satin stitched squares and then the second row of cable stitch.
- For the centre of each satin stitched square, cut four threads from each corner and withdraw them.
- Using the same needle and thread, embroider a rosette in the centre of each square.

When all the rosettes are completed the flannel flowers are embroidered. Using graph A, a flannel flower

is added to the V of each section of the doily. For this doily, I also added extra flannel flowers in each corner and in the centre as shown in the photograph. You may decide not to embroider these, but it is your choice.

- Using the cream silk ribbon and tapestry needle no. 18, embroider the petals of the flannel flower using twisted chain stitch as shown on the graph.
- When the petals are completed, change to the pale green ribbon and embroider a back stitch over the end of each of the petals.
- Embroider the centre of each flower with the pale green ribbon and six colonial knots.
- Change to coton perle no. 8 and tapestry needle no. 24 and embroider the edging using buttonhole stitch.
- Change to Buds no. 624 and embroider a row of colonial knots as placed on the graph between the second row of cable stitching and the buttonhole edging.
- Turn the embroidery to the wrong side and cut out along the buttonhole edging. Press on the wrong side with a warm iron.

DAISY DOILY

REQUIREMENTS

1 x 43 cm (17 in) square of cream Lugana
3 balls of coton perle no. 5 colour 368
1 skein Watercolour Cantelope or DMC coton perle
   no. 5 salmon
1 skein DMC stranded cotton rust
1 ball cream coton perle no. 8
1 tapestry needle no. 24
1 milliners needle no. 7

METHOD

- Starting in the centre of the fabric and graph, follow the graph and satin stitch the tulips using tapestry needle no. 24 and green coton perle no. 5.
- Count 136 fabric threads from the centre and embroider the first row of cable stitch, the satin stitched squares and then the second row of cable stitch. Also cable stitch the centre of the diamond of satin stitched squares.

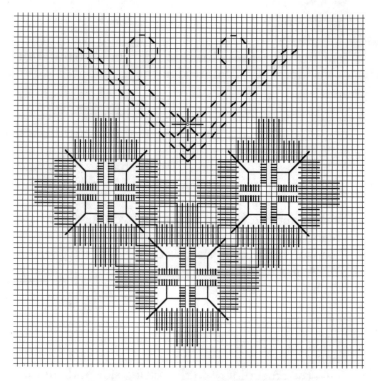

- For the centre of each satin stitched square, cut four threads from each corner and withdraw them. Using cream coton perle no. 8 and the tapestry needle no. 24, embroider a rosette in the centre of each square.
- Changing to one strand of Cantelope and the milliners needle, embroider the daisies using graph B for placement. Embroider the line of back stitching on either side of the daisy. Embroider a daisy in the corner inside the row of cable stitching.
- Changing to stranded cotton, rust, embroider a colonial knot in the centre of each of the daisies.
- Changing to green coton perle no. 5, embroider the buttonhole edging.
- Change to the Cantelope and embroider the row of colonial knots between the second row of cable stitching and the buttonhole edging.
- Turn the embroidery to the back and cut along the buttonhole edge.

Press with a warm iron.

CARDS

Daisy Card

REQUIREMENTS

1 10 cm x 14 cm (4 in x 5½ in) piece of light blue
  Jubilee
1 ball white coton perle no. 8
1 skein Minnamurra no. 8020 or DMC coton perle
  no. 8 pale blue or mauve
1 skein Minnamurra no. 20 or DMC coton perle
  no. 5 pale blue or mauve
1 skein DMC stranded 319, medium green
1 skein DMC stranded 725, dark yellow
1 tapestry needle no. 24
1 milliners needle no. 5
1 x 3 sectioned dark blue card with an oval cutout
double sided sticky tape

METHOD

● Using coton perle no. 8 and the tapestry needle no.
  24, embroider the kloster blocks which outline the

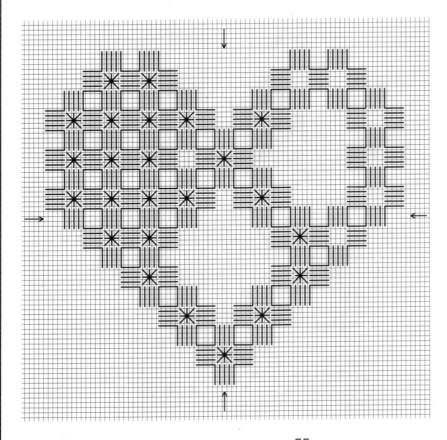

heart and then the blocks which divides the heart into sections.

- Change to Minnamurra 8020 and tapestry needle no. 24 and embroider the eyelets.
- Change to 2 strands of Minnamurra no. 20 and the milliners needle and embroider the daisy in the top right section of the heart using detached button-hole stitch.
- Change to 2 strands of DMC 319 and the same needle and embroider the stem using stem stitch and the leaves using fly stitch.
- Change to 2 strands of DMC 725 and embroider the centre of the daisy using colonial knots.
- For the spray of daisies, use 1 strand of DMC 319 and the milliners needle and embroider the stems.
- Change to 1 strand of Minnamurra 20 and the milliners needle, and embroider each of the daisies.
- Place a colonial knot in the centre of each flower using 1 strand of DMC 725 and the same needle.

When all the embroidery is complete, attach double-sided sticky tape to the front and back of the embroidery in each corner. Place it carefully under the oval of the card and centre the embroidery. Press the tape to the card. Fold in the backing piece of cardboard and press firmly.

SWEET PEA HEART CARD

REQUIREMENTS

1 10 cm x 14 cm (4 in x 5½ in) piece of blue Jubilee
1 ball white coton perle no. 8
1 skein Minnamurra no. 8020 or DMC coton perle no. 8 pale blue or mauve
1 skein Minnamurra no. 5020 or DMC coton perle no. 5 pale blue or mauve
1 skein DMC stranded 319, medium green
1 packet 2 mm pearl beads
1 tapestry needle no. 24
1 milliners needle no. 5
1 beading needle
1 x 3 sectioned white card with an oval cutout
light blue thread
double-sided sticky tape

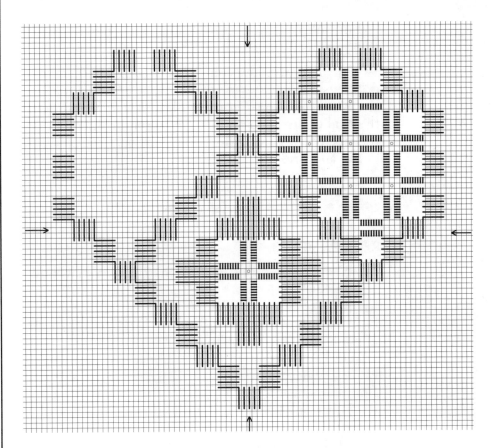

METHOD

- Using the tapestry needle and coton perle no. 8, embroider the kloster blocks which outline the heart, and then embroider the blocks which divide the heart into three sections.
- Continuing with the same needle and thread, embroider the satin stitched square and then cut four fabric threads from each corner and withdraw them. Also cut the fabric threads and withdraw them from the top right section of the heart as shown on the graph.
- Change to Minnamurra 8020 and the tapestry needle and needleweave the bars in the top right corner. Using the same thread and needle, needleweave the bars in the satin stitched square.
- In each cutwork section, attach a pearl bead where indicated on the graph using the light blue thread and the beading needle.
- Change to the milliners needle and 2 strands of Minnamurra 5020. Position the flowers as shown in the photograph and embroider the sweet peas.
- Change to two strands of DMC 319 and embroider the centre of the sweet pea bud using detached

buttonhole stitch. Embroider the stems of the flower using stem stitch.

When all embroidery has been completed, attach double-sided sticky tape to the front and back of the embroidery in each corner. Place it carefully under the oval of the card and centre the embroidery. Press the tape to the card. Fold in the backing piece of cardboard and press firmly.

ROSE CARD

REQUIREMENTS

1 x 10 cm x 14 cm (4 in x 5½ in) piece of pale pink Jubilee
1 ball white coton perle no. 8
1 skein Minnamurra no. 8050 or DMC coton perle no. 8 pale pink or yellow
1 skein DMC stranded no. 3052, medium dark green
1 tapestry needle no. 24
1 milliners needle no. 5
1 x 3 sectioned pink card with an oval cutout in the centre
double-sided sticky tape

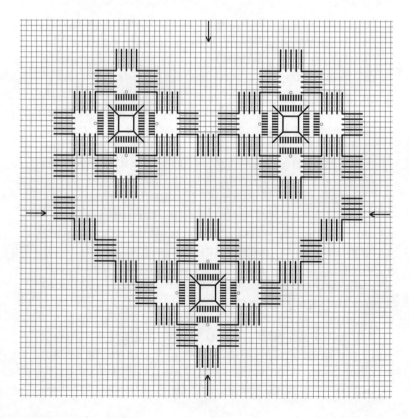

METHOD

- Using coton perle no. 8 and the tapestry needle no. 24, embroider all the kloster blocks. Cut and withdraw the fabric threads where indicated on the graph.
- Using the coton perle no. 8 and tapestry needle no. 24, needleweave the bars and embroider the square filet and the picots in each section.
- Changing to two strands of Minnamurra no. 8050 and the milliners needle no. 5, position the roses as shown in the photograph and embroider them using detached buttonhole stitch. The two outer roses have 10 wraps on the needle for the centre petal and 12 wraps for each petal in the second row. The centre rose is embroidered in the same way as the other 2 roses but also has a third row which has 12 wraps on the needle for each petal.
- Change to two strands of DMC 3052 and the milliners needle and embroider the leaves with 10 wraps on the needle for each side of the leaves.

When all the embroidery has been completed, attach double-sided sticky tape to the front and back of the embroidery in each corner. Place it carefully under the oval of the card and centre the embroidery. Press the tape to the card. Fold in the backing piece of cardboard and press firmly.

STARBURSTS

BLUE STARBURST

REQUIREMENTS

1 x 10 cm (4 in) square of cream Lugana
1 skein Spring Navy or DMC coton perle no. 5 navy
    blue
1 tapestry needle no. 24
1 beading needle
1 packet Mill Hill beads no. 00557, gold
1 packet Mill Hill bugle beads no. 72011, gold
1 gold star with a hole in the centre
cream quilting thread

METHOD

- Using the Spring Navy and tapestry needle no. 24, embroider all the kloster blocks.
- Change to the beading needle and cream quilting thread and attach a gold bead where indicated on the graph using a half cross stitch. Attach the bugle beads in the centre of the design. Attach the star in the centre of the bugle beads. Use a gold bead on top of the star to hold it in place.

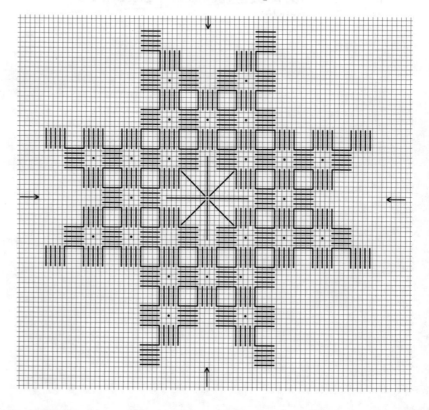

RED STARBURST

REQUIREMENTS

1 x 10 cm (4 in) square cream Lugana
1 skein Spring Lipstick Red or DMC coton perle no.
    5 bright red
1 spool DMC gold metallic thread
1 tapestry needle no. 24

METHOD

- Using Spring Lipstick Red thread and tapestry needle no. 24, embroider the kloster blocks.
- Change to the gold metallic thread and embroider
  the eyelets where indicated on the graph. Cut and
  withdraw the appropriate threads in the centre of
  the design.
- Using tapestry needle no. 24 and the metallic
  thread, needleweave the bars and the square filet
  and the picots.

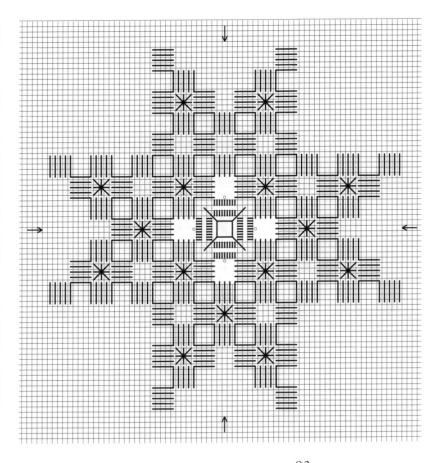

EMERALD STARBURST

REQUIREMENTS

1 x 10 cm (4 in) square of cream Lugana
1 skein Spring Emerald or DMC coton perle no. 5
   emerald green
1 spool DMC gold metallic thread
1 packet Mill Hill beads no. 00561, pale green
1 tapestry needle no. 24
1 beading needle
cream quilting thread

METHOD

- Using Spring Emerald thread and tapestry needle no. 24, embroider the kloster blocks. Cut and withdraw the appropriate threads as indicated on the graph.
- Change to gold metallic thread and tapestry needle no. 24 and needleweave the bars and the square filets and the picots.
- Change to the beading needle and cream quilting thread and attach the beads where indicated on the graph using a half a cross stitch.

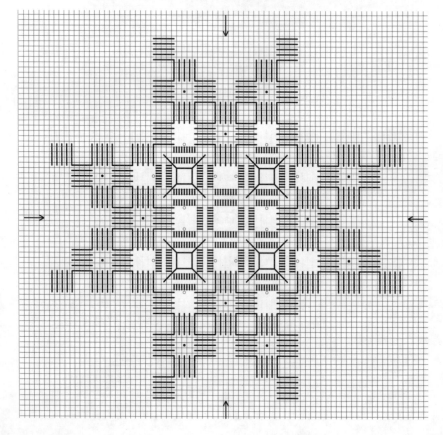

CHRISTMAS DECORATIONS

Starry Night

REQUIREMENTS

1 x 11.5 cm (4½ in) square of cream Lugana
1 skein Spring Lipstick Red or DMC coton perle no.
   5 bright red
1 packet Mill Hill beads no. 00221, bronze
8 gold stars with holes in the centre
1 tapestry needle no. 24
1 beading needle
cream quilting thread

METHOD

- Using Spring Lipstick Red and tapestry needle no. 24, embroider the diamonds using satin stitch.
- Change to the beading needle and cream quilting thread. Attach a bead in the centre of each diamond using a half cross stitch as indicated on the graph. Attach a star with a bead in the centre where indicated on the graph by the solid dots between the diamonds on the border.

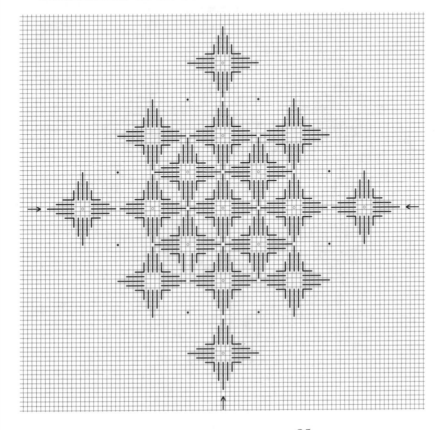

MOSAIC

REQUIREMENTS

1 x 19 cm (7½ in) square cream Lugana
1 skein Spring Navy or DMC coton perle no. 5 navy
  blue
1 packet Mill Hill beads no. 03002, blue
1 tapestry needle no. 24
1 beading needle
cream quilting thread

METHOD

- Using Spring Navy and tapestry needle, embroider the diamonds using satin stitch.
- Change to the beading needle and cream quilting thread and attach the beads where indicated on the graph using a half cross stitch.

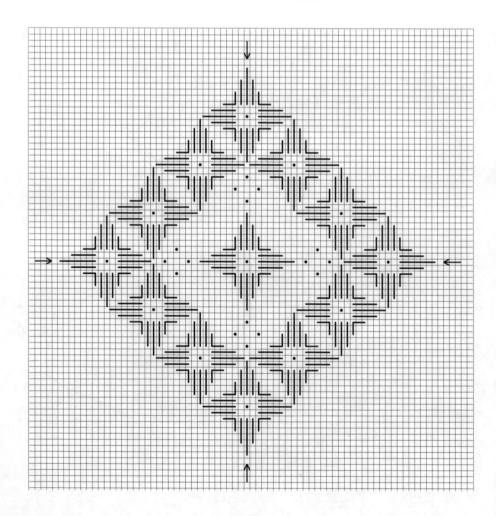

CHECKED DIAMOND

REQUIREMENTS

1 x 10cm (4 in) square of cream Lugana
1 skein Spring Lipstick Red or DMC coton perle no.
   5 bright red
1 packet Mill Hill beads no. 00221, gold
1 tapestry needle no. 24
1 beading needle
cream quilting thread

METHOD

- Using Spring Lipstick Red and tapestry needle no. 24, embroider all the kloster blocks.
- Change to the beading needle and the cream quilting thread and attach the beads with a half a cross stitch where indicated on the graph.

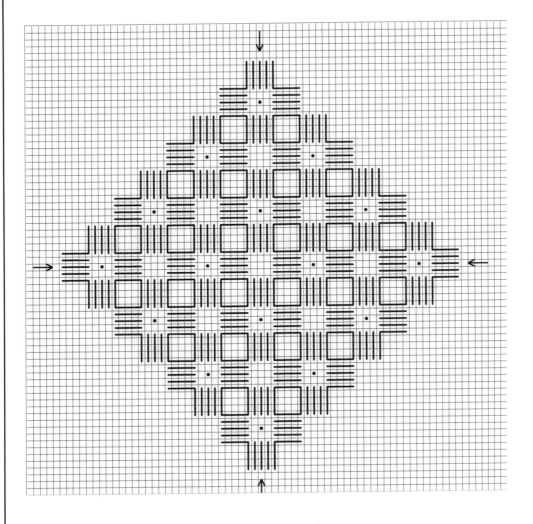

CHARM OF CHRISTMAS

REQUIREMENTS

1 x 10 cm (4 in) square of cream Lugana
1 skein Spring Navy or DMC coton perle no. 5 navy
   blue
1 heart charm 1.5 cm (⅝ in) diameter
1 packet Mill Hill beads no. 03002, blue
1 tapestry needle no. 24
1 beading needle
cream quilting thread

METHOD

- Using Spring Navy and tapestry needle no. 24,
  embroider the kloster blocks.
- Attach the beads with the beading needle and the
  cream quilting thread where indicated on the graph
  using a half cross stitch. Centre and attach the
  heart charm.

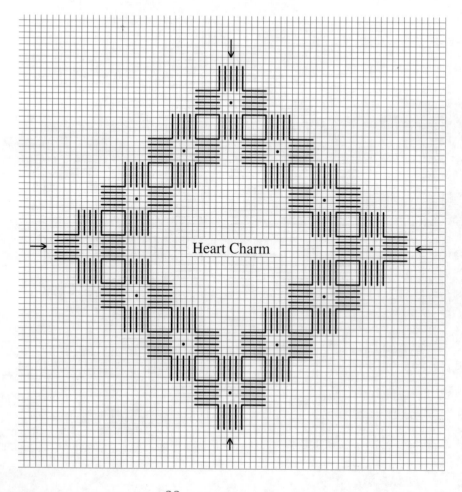

Heart Charm

STAR OF CHRISTMAS

REQUIREMENTS

1 x 12 cm (4¾ in) square of cream Lugana
1 skein Spring Lipstick Red or DMC coton perle no.
  5 bright red
1 packet Mill Hill beads no. 02013, red
1 tapestry needle no. 24
1 beading needle
cream quilting thread

METHOD

- Using Spring Lipstick Red and tapestry needle no.
  24, embroider the star in the centre using satin
  stitch. Then embroider the kloster blocks.
- Changing to the beading needle and the cream
  quilting thread, attach the beads where indicated
  on the graph using a half cross stitch.

HEARTS OF CHRISTMAS

REQUIREMENTS

1 x 10 cm (4 in) square cream Lugana
1 skein Spring Emerald or DMC coton perle no. 5
  emerald green
4 heart charms 1 cm (¼ in) diameter
1 packet Mill Hill beads no. 00557, gold
1 tapestry needle
1 beading needle
cream quilting thread

This decoration is embroidered and then turned on a 90° angle to create a diamond of embroidery instead of a square.

METHOD

- Using Spring Emerald and tapestry needle no. 24, embroider the diamonds using satin stitch.
- Changing to the beading needle and cream quilting thread, attach the beads where indicated on the graph.
- Remembering that the embroidery will be turned on an angle, centre and attach each heart charm.

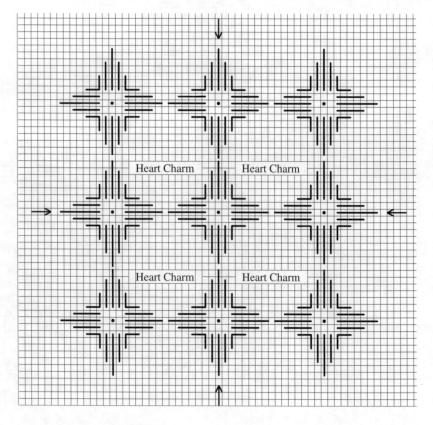

BELL

REQUIREMENTS

1 x 10 cm (4 in) square of cream Lugana
1 skein Spring Lipstick Red or DMC coton perle no.
   5 bright red
1 packet each Mill Hill beads nos. 02020 and 00221,
   green and bronze
1 packet Mill Hill bugle beads nos. 72052 and 72011,
   red and gold
2 gold stars with holes in the centre
1 tapestry needle no. 24
1 beading needle
cream quilting thread

METHOD

- Using Spring Lipstick Red and tapestry needle no.
  24, embroider the kloster blocks and the satin
  stitching.
- Changing to the beading needle and the cream
  quilting thread, attach green beads, no. 02020, in

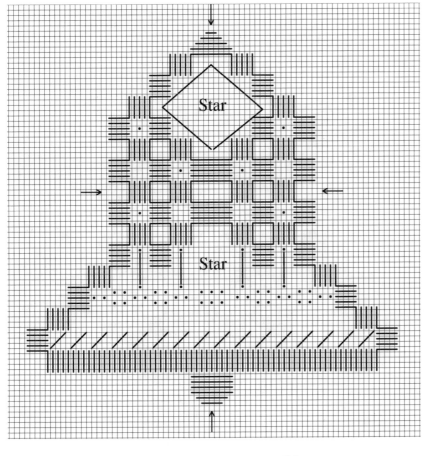

the centre of each set of kloster blocks where indicated on the graph using a half cross stitch. Attach the stars using a green bead on top of each star to hold it in place.

- Attach 8 red, no. 72052, bugle beads around the star at the top of the bell.
- Attach the red bugle beads, no. 72052, with a green bead, no. 02020, either side of the lower star where indicated on the graph.
- Attach the row of gold, no. 00221 beads, where indicated on the graph underneath the bottom star.
- Attach the row of gold, no. 72011, bugle beads across the lower edge of the bell where indicated on the graph by the diagonal lines.

LACY DIAMOND

REQUIREMENTS

1 x 10 cm (4 in) square of cream Lugana
1 skein Spring Emerald or DMC coton perle no. 5 emerald green
1 ball cream coton perle no. 8
1 packet Mill Hill beads no. 00561, pale green
1 tapestry needle no. 24

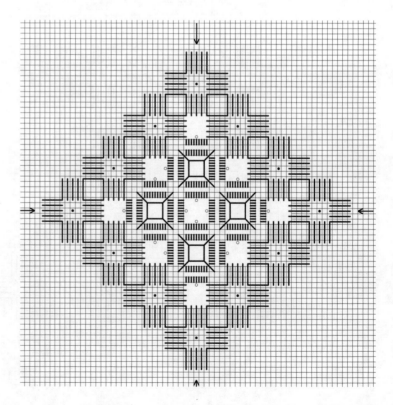

1 beading needle
cream quilting thread

METHOD

- Using Spring Emerald and tapestry needle no. 24, embroider the kloster blocks.
- Cut and withdraw the fabric threads where indicated on the graph. Change to cream coton perle no. 8 and the tapestry needle and needleweave the bars with square filets and picots.
- Change to the beading needle and the cream quilting thread and attach a bead in the centre of each set of kloster blocks where indicated on the graph using a half cross stitch.

GOLD FLOWER DIAMOND

REQUIREMENTS

1 x 10 cm (4 in) square of cream Lugana
1 skein Spring Navy or DMC coton perle no. 5 navy blue
1 spool DMC gold metallic thread
1 packet Mill Hill beads no. 03002, blue
1 tapestry needle no. 24

1 beading needle
cream quilting thread

METHOD

- Using Spring Navy and tapestry needle no. 24, embroider the kloster blocks. Cut and withdraw the fabric threads where indicated on the graph.
- Change to DMC metallic thread and the tapestry needle no. 24 and needleweave all the bars.
- Embroider the blanket stitch flower over the woven bars.
- Change to the beading needle and the cream quilting thread and attach the beads using a half cross stitch where indicated on the graph.

To Make the Christmas Decorations

REQUIREMENTS

For each decoration, a tassel is required. The instructions for making the tassel are given on page 47. Use the same thread that has been used for the embroidery in each case.

For the decorations that have lacework, a piece of fabric is required to back the embroidery. I have used a piece of cream satin.

A piece of cream Lugana the same size as the embroidered front piece.

A piece of ribbon for the hanger, 11 cm (4¼ in) long. I used a piece of silver and gold ribbon but any colour can be used.

Toy stuffing

Chenille needle, no. 18.

cream thread

sharps needle

METHOD

For the decorations that have lacework

- Cut the piece of satin to the same size as the embroidered Lugana.
- Using a 5 mm (¼ in) seam, sew the two pieces of fabric together.

For all Decorations

- Fold the ribbon for the hanger in half. Place the

embroidered Lugana face up, and then place the cut ends of the ribbon facing towards the corner and the folded end facing the centre of the embroidery. Attach the ribbon to the embroidered front of the decoration in one corner with a small straight stitch to hold it in place.

- Pin the embroidered fabric and the backing fabric right sides together. Using a 5mm (¼ in) seam, sew the two pieces together along three sides and just past the corners on the fourth side. Trim the corners and turn right side out.
- Pull the hanger into place.
- Thread the ends of the tassel through the eye of the chenille needle. Push the needle through the corner opposite the hanger and pull the ends of the tassel through to the inside of the decoration. Tie these in a knot as close to the corner as possible to secure the ends.
- Place a small amount of toy stuffing inside the decoration to pad it to the desired fullness.
- Pin the opening of the decoration together and slip stitch it together using the sharps needle and the cream thread.

FLOWER VEST

The vest pattern I have used is a patchwork pattern. I needed a pattern which had a straight edge down the front so I could embroider directly onto the vest pieces and that also did not have any darts. A jacket pattern could be used without the sleeves, or the design could be used for a jacket. The vest is also lined. It is 68.5 cm (27 in) down the edges at the front. I embroidered the two rows of the flower pattern on the fabric and then embroidered the green diamonds of Rosettes centring them between the two rows of flowers. This will vary with the size of the vest. For the back I measured the width of the front embroidery to see how it would fit across the back of the vest. I decided that I could continue the flowers and Rosettes alternating across the back. There is a small amount of black fabric on the sides which has no embroidery because of the curve of the pattern over the hips. To duplicate exactly the design I have embroidered, it may be necessary to add or decrease the number of fabric threads between each embroidery design e.g. I have 13 fabric threads from the point of the green rosettes to the triangle border. If the vest is to be wider, 20 threads at this point may be necessary.

REQUIREMENTS

1 vest pattern
1 m (1 yd) black Lugana
5 skeins Watercolour Fuchsia or DMC coton perle no. 5 dark pink
5 skeins Watercolour Abalone or DMC coton perle no. 5 sea green
4 skeins Wildflower Fuchsia or DMC coton perle no. 8 dark pink
4 skeins Wildflower Abalone or DMC coton perle no. 8 sea green
1 packet each Mill Hill beads no. 03028 pink and 03025, green
1 tapestry needle no. 24
1 beading needle
black quilting thread

METHOD
The tapestry needle no. 24 is used for all the embroidery.

- Starting at the bottom of the vertical edge on the front of the vest, and using the Wildflower Fuchsia, embroider the first row of cable stitching. Embroider 5 mm (¼ in) from the seam line.
- Change to the Watercolour Fuchsia and embroider the triangles using satin stitch.
- Using Wildflower Abalone embroider the stem of the flower.

- Change to the Watercolour Abalone and embroider the green leaves at the base of the stem using satin stitch. Also embroider the satin stitching at the top of the stem in Watercolour Abalone.
- Change to the Watercolour Fuchsia and embroider the four small buds up the stem. Then embroider the satin stitched square at the top of the stem.
- Cut and withdraw four fabric threads from each corner of the square.
- Change to Wildflower Fuschia and embroider a Rosette in the centre of the square.
- For the second row of the border, use the Wildflower Abalone and embroider the cable stitching.
- Change to the Watercolour Fuchsia and embroider the triangles using satin stitch.
- Change to the beading needle and black quilting thread and attach one bead, no. 03025, to the centre of the Rosette and in each of the pink buds using a half cross stitch. Attach a bead, no. 03028, to the centre of the green satin stitching at the top of the stem.

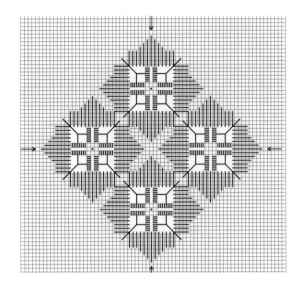

THE ROSETTES

- Using Watercolour Abalone, embroider the satin stitched squares for the Rosettes.
- Cut and withdraw four fabric threads from the corner of each square.
- Change to Wildflower Abalone and embroider a Rosette in the centre on each square.
- Change to the beading needle and black quilting thread and attach a bead, no. 03025, to the centre of each rosette using a half cross stitch.

For the pattern at the top of the vest, I measured down 14 cm or 5½ in from the lowest point of the shoulder seam and started the row of the border at this point.

- Using Wildflower Abalone and tapestry needle no. 24, embroider the row of cable stitching.
- Change to Watercolour Abalone and embroider the satin stitched triangles.
- Find the centre of the front and measure 2.5 cm (1 in) above the border embroidery and this is the starting point for the flower motif. Use the instructions above for embroidering the flower.
- Measure 5 cm (2 in) both sides of the stem of the flower and this is the starting point for the single Rosette. Use the instructions above for embroidering the Rosettes.
- Repeat the instructions above to complete the embroidery on all of the vest.
- Following the directions on your pattern, line and finish the vest.

DESIGNING YOUR OWN HARDANGER

Designing your own hardanger patterns can be a bit daunting at first but it is worth the effort. I started designing my own patterns by taking a shape from a pattern that I liked and then changing the embroidery pattern within it and sometimes the colour of the fabric as well. Also, a combination of colours can give you an idea. It took me a while to get the designs to my liking, but through trial and error, I improved. One element of designing is the use of fabric and thread as well as the amount of embroidery on each article.

The last four projects in this book are to try and help you think about designing hardanger patterns. I took a basic diamond shape of kloster blocks and put them together in various configurations and used different fabric and threads. All of these designs have been embroidered on cream or white Lugana using variegated threads.

The combination of diamonds can be an exciting challenge.

The Heart and Tulip doilies were worked combining three diamonds of kloster blocks in different configurations. The three by three diamonds work well with overall embroidery but I felt that there would have been too much embroidery if I had used the same type of design for the Roses of Autumn design which has five diamonds across it. Also, the purpose of each item has to be considered i.e. the Roses of Autumn doily has no embroidery in the centre so a vase or ornament can sit in the centre without tipping over.

Colour has an immense impact on the finished piece of embroidery. To achieve a subtle effect, i.e. the Roses of Autumn doily, a soft coloured thread has been used with a highlight of embroidered flowers. A totally different effect would have been achieved if I had used a brightly coloured thread for the single blue diamond. It is actually much brighter than the other doilies because I have used a strong blue for the embroidery on white Lugana. Light soft colours such as cream and pastels will give the embroidery a soft gentle look whereas bright colours are bold and eye catching.

I have used a combination of threads, variegated

and cream to give a lighter effect on the Heart doily. I felt that if I had used the varigated thread for all of the embroidery it would have detracted and been distracting to the design so I used cream thread for the needleweaving which then compliments the variegated thread. For the Tulips, I used a varigated thread for the complete article and left the needleweaving plain. Simplicity is always better than doing too much embroidery.

For some of the embroidery I have also added a subtle touch which can lift a piece of embroidery without overdoing it. For the Blue Diamond, I embroidered eyelets in the centre of each set of kloster blocks. For the Roses of Autumn doily, I placed a small colonial knot in the centre of each set of kloster blocks. A small bead can also be used for the same effect. A row of colonial knots was used on the Flannel Flower and Daisy doilies. I placed them between the edging and the kloster blocks. It is simple but can fill in a space easily without being out of place on the embroidery.

The style of embroidery is also important. A more solid effect can be achieved by using kloster blocks and lots of satin stitching as in the Blue Diamond. I also use needleweaving to give a lighter feeling to embroidery. With the Roses of Autumn Doily, I have featured the needleweaving in a large diamond surrounding a plain centre and then repeated the same pattern in each corner to balance the effect. I also added a few embroidered flowers in four corner blocks to complement the hardanger. Any more flowers would have been overwhelming to the overall effect of the embroidery. A balance has to be achieved with the design, colour and the amount of embroidery on each article.

I constantly try different fabrics and threads before I start a piece of embroidery to see if I can achieve the effect I am after. I often start with an idea and work with fabric and thread to see if I can achieve it. Often a combination of fabric and thread will give me a completely different idea from what I had originally envisaged. I have little samples in my cupboards of my successes as well as disasters. Like all crafts, practice and samples are useful tools for remembering what did and did not work. If it doesn't work, don't throw it away, store it along with the other pieces to make sure you don't do it again. It is only by trial and error that success is achieved.